PASSING
DOWN
THE
FARM

PASSING
DOWN
THE
FARM

The
OTHER
Farm Crisis

Donald J. Jonovic
Wayne D. Messick

JAMIESON PRESS
Cleveland

Published by JAMIESON PRESS
Post Office Box 909, Cleveland, Ohio 44120

Library of Congress Cataloging in Publication Data

Jonovic, Donald J. 1943-
Passing down the farm.
   Includes index.

1. Family farms — United States. 2. Inheritance and succession — United States. 3. Estate planning —
United States. I. Messick, Wayne D., 1944-   . II. Title.
HD1476.U5J66 1986   630′.68   86-18923
ISBN 0-915607-08-5

First Printing: September 1986

Printed in the United States of America

BUILDING THE BRIDGE FOR HIM

An old man, going on a lone highway
Came at the evening, cold and gray,
To a chasm, vast and deep and wide,
Through which was flowing a sullen tide.
The old man crossed in the twilight dim —
That sullen stream had no fears for him;
But he turned, when he reached the other side,
And built a bridge to span the tide.

"Old man," said a fellow pilgrim near,
"You are wasting strength in building here.
Your journey will end with the ending day;
You never again must pass this way.
You have crossed the chasm deep and wide,
Why build you a bridge at the eventide?"

The builder lifted his old gray head.
"Good friend, in the path I have come," he said,
"There followeth after me today
A youth whose feet must pass this way.
This chasm that has been naught to me
To that fair-haired youth may a pitfall be.
He, too, must cross in the twilight dim;
Good friend I am building the bridge for him."

Will Allen Drongoole

*For the future of the family farm
and all those who work the land
together.*

ACKNOWLEDGEMENTS

The authors would like to express their appreciation to everyone who took the time to read and comment on the manuscript in its various stages. Special thanks are due to Phyllis Slocum, and Bart & Laurel Montgomery, for editing above and beyond our call. Their contributions were a major help in our effort to make this book as meaningful and as helpful as possible.

TABLE OF CONTENTS

Preface
TROUBLE DOWN ON THE FARM

THE MACKEY FAMILY

The Problems:

- How to survive huge estate taxes
- How to bring children in fairly
- How to fund owner's retirement
- How to recognize oldest son's contribution
- How to be fair to off-farm daughter

In 1979, when we first met them, Harold and Helen Mackey had three sons and a daughter, all of them almost grown. Their son, Greg, a graduate of Penn State with a degree in agriculture, was working on the farm. Dave and Tim were still at Penn State, also in agriculture. Amy was planning on studying retailing at the same school.

It was a close and happy family. The farm business was doing well, but Harold had a number of concerns.

How, he wondered, could he prevent the forced sale of the farmland in his estate? The late 70's were a period of high inflation, combined with an estate tax structure that threatened to wipe out 50% of his estate after he and Helen died.

Land values and taxes weren't his only concern, however. He also wondered how he and Helen could safely bring the boys into the business? He wanted their work to fund his retirement, a payback, in a sense, for the years he spent raising them and putting them through school. This was his plan, but there was nothing formal to it. He sure didn't have any kind of retirement plan.

He felt his life was getting more complicated every day. Greg was married and was starting a family, which was another concern. Harold knew that priorities, even loyalties, changed when a family arrived, and Greg would soon be looking more to the future — and needing more from the farm. Tim and Dave had no plans to get married, but Harold knew time and biology would probably change that.

His sons were his successors. All through high school and college, the boys had worked on the farm, a large Indiana vegetable operation with more than 850 acres of potatoes, with additional acreage devoted to squash, cabbage, onions, sweet corn, etc.

Greg, as the oldest, had worked the longest and had been the person raising the onions. Harold made this Greg's enterprise and had created a very business-like relationship between the two of them for this project. Greg had been successful, but, as usual, success created a problem. Greg's salary over the past several years hadn't reflected the success he'd achieved, and as a result he'd taken out $90,000 less than he'd earned. He'd just left that money in the business. How, Harold wondered, could he recognize this contribution without developing a massive income tax bill? Greg still didn't need or want the cash, but that would change very soon.

The boys, to put the problem in another way, weren't equal with respect to the farm, their talents, and what they'd contributed. How, Harold wondered, could he bring them in and recognize their varying contributions without penalizing them for the fact that Greg was born first?

Finally, he wondered what to do about Amy. She clearly was not a farmer, and didn't seem to ever want to be one. Furthermore, she had her sights set on the "big time" in retailing. There wasn't a chance that she would marry a farmer, much less come back to live on the farm. (SOLUTIONS OUTLINED IN THE POSTSCRIPT) . . .

THE PAUL FAMILY

The Problems:

- How to handle too many interested heirs
- How to recognize oldest son's contribution
- How to handle explosive growth in business value

Garth and Ruth Paul faced a serious dilemma. They had five boys, two long-term fears about the succession of their farm, and an uncomfortable answer.

Their first fear was that, after all of their work and sacrifice, none of the boys would be interested in being a farmer. Their second fear, equally serious, was that all five of their sons would want to be involved in the farm, and they didn't believe that the farm would or could support five families. By 1980, it was becoming obvious that Fear #2 was the more valid of the two.

Tom, their oldest, had been working on the farm for several years. Kevin, who at that time was living in Seattle and working as a draftsman, was hinting that he wanted to come back to the farm. Their third son, Ron, was almost finished with high school and was growing more interested in farming. The youngest two, Jeff and Denny, didn't know what they wanted to do, but a trend was certainly establishing itself. Garth and Ruth could guess where things were headed.

They were worried, and probably because of that worry, they hadn't been able to plan for a transfer of the business. It had always been a one-man show. Garth had always operated the business as a sole proprietor, and was paying Tom an hourly wage. Tom was the only son who'd really worked on the farm.

The others had been limited to the usual chores and odd jobs. Now, the Pauls feared, if they brought one or two of the other boys into the business, wouldn't that dilute the time and effort already spent by Tom? And yet, the other boys should have a chance.

There was this problem of room. Could the farm absorb everyone? Oh, Garth was talking about turning over the reins to the boys, but this by itself was setting up some conflicts in his mind. He was only 55. He thought he should retire to give the young Turks some room, but he really didn't want to, not if he was truthful with himself. He loved farming. Yes, he felt he should be making some sort of transition happen, but he didn't know how to put it together — or *where he would go if he did.*

Meanwhile, the business was getting bigger and bigger all the time — much bigger than he'd ever expected it to be — and, in 1980, BIG translated into a big *problem.*

The value of the farmland was rising rapidly. The Pauls were involved in the fruit business and had thousands of young fruit trees. Even though land in the state of Washington had generally declined in value, their land promised to increase significantly with the maturing of the trees and the beginning of full production. (SOLUTIONS OUTLINED IN THE POST-SCRIPT) . . .

THE LEBERT FAMILY

The Problem:

- How to handle the lack of interested heirs

Russell and Lois Lebert were in their early 60's. They had two children and a fruit operation that was prospering. But it didn't look like the children and the farm would ever come together.

Their daughter, Linda, had married and moved away. She and her husband were teachers, and only came home each summer as part of their vacation to do some work in the orchards, mostly because they enjoyed working out of doors. They were great helpers during the time of year that they were available, and took charge of several areas during the harvest, but their involvement only amounted to two or three weeks each year.

Their son, Chris, was developing into a mechanical genius. During his growing years, he would always work on the machinery — the cherry shakers, the tractors, etc. That he loved. Farming, he really could do without.

Russell had seen this talent some years before and had built Corn Belt Equipment Company on some land the farm owned near a major state highway. The company handled several lines of farm machinery and became well known in their section of the state for business expertise and the ability to maintain the equipment.

As a result, Corn Belt Equipment was a booming enterprise under Chris, and the Lebert orchards were left without a successor for the next generation. (SOLUTIONS OUTLINED IN THE POSTSCRIPT) . . .

THE GRANGERS

The Problems:

- How to handle ownership transfer to cousins
- How to handle different numbers of heirs between owning families

Jack and Dale owned a large vegetable business, with more than 2000 acres of miscellaneous crops, including 300 acres of asparagus. It was one of the largest such operations in Wisconsin.

The two brothers had worked together for more than 45 years, having started out together in high school when their father gave them each a hog and sold them the corn to feed it. From that initial beginning, they bought more livestock, sold it and ultimately began to buy land. All of the land that they owned they owned together, and they had purchased it all. None was inherited. As a matter of fact, even though they were close to

60 when we met them, their father was still alive and still owned his own farm. These were truly self-made individuals.

Because of their different personalities, Jack and Dale were able to operate together very well over the years. Each took on a different role in the operation so there was no duplication of effort. However, with the arrival of the next generation of ownership (both of them were married and had family members involved in the family farm business), they worried that they'd be forcing their children to work together. They were afraid this might not be fair to those children.

They believed their children to be substantially different personalities from their fathers. Jack had three children, two girls and a boy. His two daughters, Donna and Gail, were in their early 20's and single. They worked on the farm "in season," but had no long-term commitment at the time. The son, Rick, was very much involved in the business and was the leading contender for the head of the operation in the next generation.

Dale's son, Buck, at the time we began working on the transition plan, was just finishing high school and, like his Dad, was a hard worker but showed no interest in the operating side of the business. Dale's daughter went to beauty school and owned a beauty shop in the small town close by. She had no interest in the operation whatever.

One problem that had to be dealt with was the fact that Rick would end up with ⅓ of his father's portion of the business while Buck would end up with ½ of his family's. Depending on how things were set up, Buck could ultimately own more of the business than Rick, and this wasn't necessarily in everybody's best interest. (SOLUTIONS OUTLINED IN THE POST-SCRIPT) . . .

Chapter 1
THE "OTHER" FARM CRISIS

America's farms are in crisis.

There's nothing new in this statement. Nothing unexpected. Press reports, magazine articles, government studies are all filled with sorrowful statistics about the precarious situation faced by our more than 2 million family farms.

But exactly what is the "crisis"?

Right off, some people will say it's imaginary. There's no problem, they believe, for the majority of farmers. Consider these facts:[1]

> 1) *Average farm income in 1983 was $24,090.*

> 2) *Total farm income rose almost 30% between 1983 and 1984.*

> 3) *Farm population decrease is nothing new. In fact, the loss of 43,000 farms in 1984 should be compared to an average annual loss of 123,000 farms between 1961 and 1963.*

4) *Debt-ridden farms are relatively rare.
More than 82% of all farms have debt/asset ratios
less than 40%, with 10% or less being very common. These are manageable ratios.*

5) *More than 95% of farmers were able
to get financial aid for planting in 1985, and only
1.36% of farms were reported by the USDA to be
insolvent.*

So, is there no problem at all? Of course there is. Folks
aren't just *imagining* all the farm auctions. The suffering of our
neighbors is very real. Some farmers are suffering, and most
people in agriculture would have to be blind not to see that.

But the problems are not the epidemic some ask us to
believe.

TODAY'S PROBLEMS ARE LIMITED

According to the Farmbank Research Service in Denver,
those who are under the most stress are the "medium-sized"
farms (with between $40,000 and $500,000 in annual sales) who
have debt/asset ratios greater than 40%. This is about 9% of
all the nation's operators.[2]

Their problem?

Certainly, part of it is lack of cash. Farm prices are uncertain, out of the farmer's control in most cases, and generally
depressed. Borrowing on the assets has become more difficult.
Land values, which used to rival those vast black pools of oil
under foreign deserts, have been dropping since 1980.

Once, you could describe the farmer as land rich and
money poor. Today's farmer is just as likely to be land poor, too.

Some family farms, suffering under low market prices,
high interest rates, and a steady decline in supports and sub-
sidies have become little more than a pipeline, carrying cash
between the banks and the suppliers. What cash remains in the
cookie jar comes mostly from off-farm income.

Virgil Thompson, President of the Ohio Farmers Union,
said in 1985 that 40% of his farmers faced bankruptcy. Almost

a fifth of his members had debt-to-asset ratios greater than 44%.

"I get mad," he said, *"When I see our people produce record crops and then they can't pay
their bills."*

This crushing debt structure isn't static, either. Many
farm owners went into heavy debt in the 70's when flexible interest rates were around 7%. Since then, they've faced cash-
devouring rates in the double digits.

*Still, only 9% or 10% of our farms are actually facing
the auction block.* Certainly, the situation is distressing for those
involved. But don't the statistics also suggest that we should stop
wringing our hands for a moment and look at the other 90% or
so, to see how things are going for them?

That's exactly what we've chosen to do — to look at the
future of the *successful* operations to see what clouds and storms
they face. We believe the successful family farm is critical to
America's future, and it's heartening to report that the outlook
is positive.

TOMORROW'S PROBLEMS ARE SERIOUS

The opportunities are great for the present farm owners
and their heirs, but the horizon is also clouded by the question
of *long-term* survival: Will the 90% of today's farms that are
solvent successfully pass down to tomorrow's farmers?

This is the *other* farm crisis, a less visible, but a most
important problem that raises serious questions whether the farm
can, in fact, be passed down from today's owners to the next
generation.

To understand the nature of this problem, it's necessary
to understand the uniqueness of the family farm as a business,
a business that's very different even from the family farm of
just a generation ago.

Farming has always followed its own set of business
standards. It's a different breed of business with a unique four-
phase history as an industry.

The *first phase* was the era of the strong back. During these years, the farmer and his mule worked the fields by hand. Back then, a farmer's success was often determined by how long he could walk behind a plow and how many straight 20-hour days he could work without dropping into the furrows.

Then came the *second phase*, with the development of the steel-bottomed plow, the mechanical threshing machines and the like. This was the era of machinery. Well, *agriculture*, as an industry, entered the machinery era — but not all farmers. Many just couldn't make the transition, because . . . well, you just can't talk to a tractor the way you can talk to the mules. Some people just couldn't get used to machinery.

Those farmers are now gone, as are their farms, absorbed by those who mechanized.

The *third phase* arrived with the introduction of chemicals and biology into farming, introductions which created a revolution in productivity. Chemicals allowed for the control of diseases and weeds while, at the same time, the botanists and agricultural biologists were creating stronger animal breeds and varieties of plants which ripened quicker, could be harvested later, and withstood more unusual or extreme conditions. This combination resulted in tremendous productivity.

This was a good thing. With the traditionally low level of farm prices, the only way to be profitable was to be more productive using this new technology. Still, many farmers couldn't make the transition.

Those farmers are now gone, their farms absorbed by their neighbors who could adapt to scientific agriculture.

FARMING HAS BECOME A BUSINESS

And now agriculture is entering a *fourth phase*, perhaps the most revolutionary of all. It's our belief, and the belief of most experts in the agricultural community, that *to succeed in the 80's and 90's, today's farmers are going to have to run their farms more and more like the businesses they are.* No matter how romantic are the images called up by "the family farm," today's successful farm is, first and foremost, a *business* — in many cases, a very big business.

But, to repeat ourselves, the family farm is unique as a business. The net worth of the typical farm is usually very high, for example, but the gross income that net worth supports is typically very low. It's not unusual for a net worth of $1 million to generate a mere $25,000 annual income. And that income barely covers Mom and Dad.

Cash income, although generally low and uncertain, is not the only difficulty, however. While cash problems do account for the most commonly recognized farm crisis, the "other crisis" this book addresses affects far more family farms. It's source is a combination of difficulties, part family, part who-gets-what-and-how.

Think about the realities for the family in farming. The return on investment of a farm is typically so limited that no non-operator would want to own it. Owner-operators at least get a range of non-cash "perks" that can make it all worthwhile. But this makes the farm almost worthless to off-farm heirs.

Why? Because there's nothing in it for them. A family farm's balance sheet and income statements are almost reversed from what most people accept as normal for a business. A machine tool company in Chicago might be able to afford unemployed heirs in St. Louis, because it's using $2 million of assets to develop $50 million in sales. That can provide a source of cash to pay off the outsiders through buy-out or dividends. Not so the family farm, where there's usually much investment and not much return.

The off-farm owners (or potential owners) are as smart as the operators. They get (or will get) little for their shares, and they know it. Sure, the typical in-town business has cash problems, too, but the problem is usually much more severe on the family farm — causing troubles within the farm family that go far beyond mere money worries.

These concerns define the other farm crisis — the great financial and personal difficulties involved with passing it all down from generation to generation.

While the farm is valued as a way of life, it's become more than simply a way of making a living. Today's financial realities have turned the farm into an investment, and new questions are arising. Is it a business? If so, how will it survive, under whose direction and to whose benefit?

And even prior to these questions there's a more fundamental one: Can the *family* survive success in farming?

THE ANSWER: A PLAN FOR PASSING IT DOWN

We don't pretend to have all the answers. Anyone who does is outright insensitive or a downright fraud. But we do know that thousands of family farms have done the job right — farms owned by people like the Mackeys, the Pauls, the Leberts and the Grangers described in the beginning of this book. From them, and people like them, we can learn some of the approaches and techniques that work financially, but also work personally, in ways everyone can accept as just and fair.

The solutions to farm succession problems — be they family or financial — are essentially simple in concept. They involve understanding the true nature of the situation, then getting going on some thorough and practical planning. These are the subjects of this book.

We've developed a list of the essential components of a working plan for passing down the farm. In every farm family where succession was handled smoothly and positively, each of these components was carefully thought through, developed, and successfully carried out. If any one of them is missing or poorly handled, the dream of smooth transition is almost sure to become a nagging nightmare.

If a family farm is going to be truly successful — growing, profitable, and, above all, a happy place to work, year after year, generation after generation — this is what must happen:

1) *Because children of successful people will have more assets than their parents did, these "rich" kids (as the folks in-town see them) will have to be taught how to survive their dangerous opportunity.*

2) *Their spouses have to be integrated into the family as they arrive — a sometimes painful, but necessary, process.*

3) *A long-range plan must be developed — "long-range" meaning farther ahead than next weekend.*

4) *The plan must be followed — but it must allow enough flexibility to change as the world changes.*

5) *Farm heirs have to be brought into the ownership process in ways more formal than chance and more sensitive than probate.*

6) *A plan and funding vehicle for management and ownership transition must be available — in writing (uncomfortably concrete though that might be for the present owners).*

7) *The present owner(s) must have realistic and practical things to do when the plan inevitably calls for them to let go.*

8) *Some outside body, call it an advisory council, an outside board, a management "cabinet," or what you will, must be given responsibility for all of the above — and its members must have the talent, energy, commitment, and courage to do the job.*

This kind of planning, not liquidation, or mega-farming, or a separation of family and business, is the real road to success as a farm-owning family. Management and ownership of a successful family farm is often difficult and sometimes unpleasant, but like growing old, it's infinitely preferable to the alternative.

It's true that sometimes the stresses of farming lead to alcoholism or divorce, or desertion. It's true that the dawn-to-dusk (and beyond) work schedule can lead to the neglect of our children, crippling accidents, and sickness. It's also possible that disagreements will result in brothers who don't talk, parents and children who are frustrated with each other, in-laws who feel cut off and cut out, and sometimes even down-and-out courtroom battles.

But these disasters don't have to occur. They aren't inevitable.

There are ways we can learn to talk to each other without explosions.

There *are* ways to recognize the difference between disagreements about facts and disagreements about values — and to react reasonably to each.

There *are* ways to get along with daughters-in-law and sons-in-law.

There are ways to plan for liquidity, to be fair to farm and off-farm heirs alike, to organize for growth, and to get quality help and advice.

There are ways to separate labor and management, and to differentiate ownership from control.

There are ways to pass it down without giving it away. There are ways for the owner to teach, to stay in control while passing on equity and dividing the labor of working the farm. There are ways to put together an integrated financial plan.

There are ways to be fair with the kids. Ownership can be discussed in different terms with different offspring. There are many ways to divide it up so ownership and control are different issues. Classes of ownership can be created so the farm can be given, willed, or sold to farm heirs, or bought by them from the off-farm heirs, so that years of effort by the new generation will be recognized in their form of ownership.

There are ways, and they must be followed.

We believe that a successful family farm provides one of the most exciting economic opportunities one can have in our society, and we know from experience that it is, in fact, possible to benefit from that opportunity.

---

[1]Donald Lambro, Columnist, United Features Syndicate, 1985.
[2]"Financial Stress Not Shared by all Farmers," *The Drovers Journal*, December 5, 1985, p. 10.

Chapter 2
THE REAL PROBLEMS: FAMILY, AND GIVING IT AWAY

There's a great temptation to apply hard-nosed invest-ment criteria to the family farm. Particularly in an era of "free market" economics, profit could easily be used as the only meas-ure to determine the worth and merit of a family farm. Pro-ductivity, in fact, seems to be related directly to size, so bigger is better. Right?

Well, if that's so, what do we need family farms for, any-way? The statistics are clear, the largest farms achieve the big-gest margins.

To a number cruncher, this all might sound good, but it's really a form of financial tunnel vision. The fact is — a fact learned in the in-town business years ago — that economies of scale at some point fade in the face of the effort and commitment of the owner-manager. Do the statistics on economy of scale really take into account the kind of asset the "family" in "family farm" represents? Isn't it possible that the large operations, run by absentee owners, won't be able to reach their expected pro-ductivity, while the smaller, family-managed operations will?

We firmly believe that there's more to this farm crisis issue than profit margins. There are other equally important factors that are somewhat fuzzy, perhaps, but powerful nevertheless. In the words of Justin Isherwood, who farms 1,100 acres in Plover, Wisconsin:

> *"Americans instinctively want to preserve the spiritual values of farming and the heritage of the soil, but our reluctance to admit that has led to a series of ill-conceived programs that have not kept small farmers independent but rather fostered overproduction and dependence on Washington's largesse."*

WHAT'S SO HOT ABOUT THE FAMILY FARM?

Farm ownership, like entrepreneurship in general, is one of our last frontiers. It beckons irresistibly to our rugged individuals, compulsive pioneers, and incurable heroes. There's a certain romance, too, in owning one's own farm.

Sure, some grizzled old veterans — successful, but beaten-up by years under a fickle sky — might "hummpf!" at this idea of "romance." It's tough, hard, dirty work, they would say. Don't go building it up into more than it is.

These same grumps, though, after a few cold beers or a beautiful harvest sunset, will easily spin yarn after yarn about "the good old days." Fact is, most of them, if they had the chance to do it all over again, probably would.

What gets in the way isn't lack of cash, or bad weather, or "greedy" banks. What gets in the way is that many "successful" farm families at some point loose the fundamental component of the success formula. Far too many define success like this:

$$[+] + [\$] = \textbf{SUCCESS}$$

But that's not the full equation. Growth, $[+]$, and profit, $[\$]$, are essential, sure, but they're not enough. In our mind, and in the minds of our clients who are *truly* successful, the formula looks more like this:

$$[+] + [\$] + \textbf{FUN} = \textbf{SUCCESS}$$

Am I successful? Well, my operation is growing and we're making some money. But am I successful?

Not, from our point of view, unless doing it all is fun.

"Fun," as used here, doesn't mean "playing." It means enjoyment. It means feeling like we want to get to it every morning, and happy we did it every night. It means taking pleasure in working with other family members, because they're people we love and trust. It means sharing problems and joys. It means knowing *for sure* that what we're building is adding to the future and security of those we love.

For many fortunate families this ultimate success is real. But it's not true for all. In fact, for the majority of successful family farms, true success remains as maddeningly elusive as a balanced national budget.

MANAGING THE FAMILY

Here we come across the keystone of our "other" farm crisis: the difficulty farm families have in organizing and taking advantage of their primary asset, themselves.

The prospect of owning a family farm is a promised joy, but like most such dreams, the family farm has a weakness that only becomes apparent when real people try to live it.

And what is this weakness?

The family. The very source of the farm's greatest strength can also be its weakest link — and this is true whether or not all of the cash and liquidity problems have been worked out.

Maybe this sounds like a contradiction, but it's a fact that many people who are *in* family farms see their families as roadblocks, not assets. Often, they're forced by this way of looking at things into trying to separate family concerns from farm problems, a desire that seems particularly common and strong among

The Kids, the inheriting generation.

Instead of reveling in the advantages of family owner-ship, many people want to divorce family life from business life. In fact, many of these misguided clans have *policies* that busi-ness will *not* be discussed at family gatherings. Others, who don't have such policies, sometimes wish they did as another family Thanksgiving rolls around and the usual business "discussion" heats up over yet another cooling turkey.

This all too common "divorce-wish" is the result of a widespread carelessness among families who operate their own farms. They fail to treat their families as the assets they really are.

These "divorce prone" people aren't antisocial. They're normal, nice people suffering from emotional confusion, frus-tration, conflicting goals, apathy, and disappointment. In spite of their financial success, and despite the fact that they've worked together for years, they find themselves aching to back away from a partnership that was once among the most attractive rea-sons for working on the family farm.

Farm ownership can be like sailing in rough weather. The wind and the speed are exhilarating, but only if you're in con-trol. With the family involved intimately in the operation, the deck can get crowded with a sometimes unruly mob. It's bad enough when the crew isn't organized to work together, but it can get downright dangerous when people start fighting over control of the helm.

Small wonder everybody starts dreaming about solitude and peace.

Families who own farms travel together, out in some pretty rough weather. They do it day after day, season after season. It's tough to be stoic — let alone enthusiastic — when your own crew seems determined to turn you broadside to the waves. For those farming families who manage themselves well, the journey can be an enticing, if risky, challenge. For those who are poorly organized, however — as far too many are — the experience can be hell.

You'd think success would make all this easier, but you'd

be wrong. Success is too often measured solely in terms of growth and profit. But that kind of success brings as many problems — to everybody in the family — as it solves. As time goes by, the people who need each other the most find it harder and harder to get along. Because they forgot the most important reason for working together, they accepted the fact that they no longer enjoyed what they did.

WHY OLD DAD'S SO TOUGH

For the owner (usually Dad, but males have no monopoly on agriculture), owning a farm can be tough. It's also risky — and the uncertainties never really disappear, no matter how successful he becomes.

Farmers — even the successful ones — wake up "unemployed" every morning of their working lives. They know if they don't get out there and work, every day, nobody else will. They teeter precariously from crisis to crisis, far above the relative security of a real job. There are no safety nets, and all success tends to do is raise their personal highwire further off the ground.

This is why successful farm owners are so crusty. It's living with this uncertainty that underlies their uncompromising tenacity, pride, and drive. They know what it's like to lie awake in three a.m. "blink" sessions, staring at the all-too-familiar crack in the bedroom ceiling, wondering how they'll get through the coming day, much less to the harvest. The immediate problems may vary, but the underlying fears are the same.

The experience teaches The Boss one thing for sure — there's only one person who can get him across his tightrope.

Who, you ask?

Hizzoner, of course: Dad, himself.

Each farm owner "learns" during the early years that there's nobody he can depend on but himself, and maybe his family. So he's tough. He's resourceful. And he's alone.

No question, the owner of a successful family farm has a lot going for him. He's a noticeably self-contained breed — and proud of it. But that also means he cuts himself off from many potential allies, including his own family. Because of the struggles, he keeps an emotional distance that contradicts one of the major reasons he stayed in farming in the first place — providing opportunity for his family.

Listen for a minute to one of his "blink" sessions:

> *"I'm really tired. Got to start taking it easier. But who's going to run the farm? I don't think the kids can afford it, but I can't simply give it to them. Besides, what would I do with myself — and where would I get the cash to do it? And why does my son's wife bug me so much . . ."*

Assuming he hasn't been totally exhausted by his life, assuming he still cares, worries like these will inevitably flap around him in the dark, in ever-expanding circles. How will the farm survive, he wonders, if his children can't afford to buy it from him, or from each other for that matter? What about his off-farm heirs? What about his own security, and his wife's — and what happens to a farmer who's worked all his life if he suddenly stops?

The Boss suffers all this in silence, of course, (recall how tough he is), but his isn't the only suffering. Dad's stiff (actually "quivering") upper lip, unknown to him, is being imitated in other dark bedrooms around the county by other members of his family.

They, too, lie awake at three a.m. They wonder why Dad is so stubborn and secretive. They wonder why he doesn't talk to them and why working the farm isn't the fun it used to be, or why their marriages are suddenly so explosive. Why, they wonder, is it harder and harder to get up in the morning? Why do the slightest disagreements become major blowouts? And why isn't the family close anymore?

THE SIDE EFFECTS OF SUCCESS

Year after year, people on family farms tend to draw further apart. They watch in confusion as the primary blessing of farm ownership seems to slip away into a fog of frustration and disagreement.

This is a side effect of success felt only by the insiders. The outside world sees the farm as "undeserved" wealth and "unwarranted privilege" (after all, his dad "gave" it to him, didn't he?), but, inside, the participants hardly enjoy the so-called benefits. Instead, they continuously chew on indigestible problems. They worry them like a dog does a sliver in his paw. They carry these problems home. They carry them out to the barns, the fields, and the orchards. They carry them everywhere they go — and they each carry them *alone*.

How, they ask themselves, did nice people like us get into a situation like this?

Far too many successful family farms suffer this way — isolated, inbred islands of discontent and confusion. It needn't happen, but as long as it does, days, months, and years will be wasted while the strength of the business slowly leaks away.

For a family farm to maintain success from generation to generation, the existence of the family has to be accepted, worked with, and used to advantage. Family is an asset, no less than the more tangible assets listed on the balance sheet, and it must be treated as such.

Nobody pours as much energy, commitment, sweat, and funds into a farming operation as do the owners of that farm.

THE "GIVING IT AWAY" PROBLEM

Even if we assume that the farm family can learn to work together and take more benefit than pain from success, however, the "other" crisis still hasn't been solved. There remains a silo full of financial, legal and technical problems to be solved. This remaining portion of the "other crisis" is not a question of cash flow, exactly. It's a crisis of *liquidity*, caused by the need to assure the existence of a large enough dollar reservoir to handle the sudden drain on cash that occurs at the death of a principal owner.

In the past, the land was simply handed down. But since

the farm didn't have much value other than the underlying assets, it could be left entirely to the next generation without much problem. Today, even though values have slid — in some cases severely — they are still significantly greater than they were when the present generation took over.

Typically, between 70% and 80% of the net assets of the farm owner are tied up directly in the farm business, and, because of this, most farms don't have the many thousands of dollars needed to solve the problems of transfer costs and taxes. When death occurs, the cash is locked solidly in machinery, equipment, land, livestock, chemicals, tree stock, and all the other assets needed to run the farm.

One farm owner we know had $200,000 in retained earnings. When it was suggested that he earmark that money to pay transfer costs and taxes, he responded that his retained earnings were essential as working capital.

> *"We need that money every year,"* he exclaimed, *"to get the crop out!"*

Fact is, it's a rare farm today that will be large enough to sell off fixed assets — land, for example — to pay transfer costs and taxes, and still have the operating cash to stay in business. This is particularly true if the previous owner has reached the Heavenly Harvest.

Could you write a check for 30% or 40% of your net worth today? In effect, that's what the executor may have to do, and if he can't, he's going to have to think about liquidating assets. This is why liquidity planning is vital.

The severity and pervasiveness of this problem was set in bold face by columnist Mike Lafferty in 1983. To paraphrase his concern: times must be hard on the farm if the vice president of the Future Farmers of America doesn't want to be a farmer.

More accurately, he *couldn't* be a farmer. In 18-year-old Bruce Kettler's words:

> *"There's no way I can get the capital. It's too huge an investment."*

Lack of liquidity can cause serious income problems. If the executor has to raise money by liquidation, obviously he's going to be forced to liquidate the assets that are most saleable. And which assets are the most saleable? Those that produce income, like the land, securities, and other marketable holdings. Fine. But these assets are the ones that provide the income for the family.

Thus begins the downward spiral.

Don't forget. Dad's gone. Mother is alone and worried (she's always been worried in the past, so how can she not worry now?).

The nest egg has been used to pay the government, and a new generation is in charge of the farm.

The son wants to prove himself, to expand the business.

The daughter wants her money, because her oldest child is ready for college.

The daughter-in-law has sacrificed all these years, but she's not from a farm background, so she doesn't know that you're supposed to sacrifice FOR LIFE. She wants to buy some of the things her in-town friends have. Why not? She's seen the books — the farm had gross sales of $500,000 last year. What's the problem?

And Mom worries some more. How can she satisfy everyone, yet still be secure and have money as long as she needs it?

This bleak picture is all too common in farms that have experienced the death of an owner without a viable plan for passing down the farm. But there is another way: *write that plan*.

Understanding what's needed to put such a plan together, and finding the tools and people to help us plan, are, essentially, what the rest of this book is about.

Chapter 3
GRANDDAD AND DAD — TROUBLES BEGIN AT HOME

The Family Farm *is* going to survive, despite the gloomy predictions of some of the experts. We've seen too many of them succeed in the face of what seemed like overwhelming odds to believe otherwise.

Still, many farms won't survive.

And we have to ask why.

Today's farm owner is fighting heavy financial pressures most in-town business owners under 60 probably wouldn't re-member — if, indeed, they ever experienced them at all. The modern farmer's in the midst of an economic upheaval that's likely to keep hanging on like a mad badger with lockjaw.

But it's hard to overemphasize one fact: the current problems aren't solely financial. They go much deeper, attack-ing the very roots of independent farming. Economic conditions just don't explain all of the problems facing the family farmer, just as they've never explained all the problems of the in-town business.

There's more to the farm crisis than depressed prices,

government policy, or trade deficits. These can stick the last straw into an already weakened or wounded operation, of course, but they are not necessarily the fundamental nor the only cause of family farm failures.

There is a second fact to consider: there exist some internal factors — factors of human relationships, organization, management, and planning — that have a strong impact on survival or failure, and they are the principal components of what we refer to as the "other" farm crisis.

The family farm will not disappear. It may rearrange itself economically. Larger farms may absorb smaller farms. Efficient operations will eclipse the inefficient. The farms with the weakest balance sheets will be unable to weather the debt crisis.

In the end, though, many family farms will remain. There will be survivors of today's agricultural "depression," just as there were survivors of the Great Depression of the 30's.

But then, you may ask, if economic crisis isn't necessarily terminal, what makes the difference? Well, we believe strongly that the more serious challenges lie beyond the economic causes of failure or, more accurately perhaps, *behind* them, in the farm family itself.

Here, we find the "other" farm crisis.

HARVESTING WHAT GRANDDAD SOWED

The "modern" family farm is really only semi-modern. It still carries within itself structural seeds sown many years ago by Granddad when he got the whole thing going.

Some of what he sowed accounts for the strength and success of the farm business that evolved. But his seed wasn't totally clean. Mixed with the main crop are sprouting, ancestral weeds that tend to overwhelm the "modern" crop, much the way that Godzilla-like vine, kudzu, can overwhelm a roadside phone booth.

Maybe nobody ever bothered to hang an oil portrait of old Gramps over the mantle, but his spirit is around, even though he, himself, is long gone. His legacy is a fine one, to be sure, but its blessings come with some very sharp and pointed edges.

Although Granddad's heirs face modern worries he never knew, they've also inherited his way of managing them.

We might *talk* about "modern" farming. Today's family farm has draped the "ag business" cloak around its shoulders, and has even developed all of the more familiar characteristics of the in-town business. It's "organized," "monitored," "managed," "planned," "reviewed" — all that sort of thing. Income is measured almost solely in dollars, with "return on investment" becoming ever more visible as a measure of success.

Sometimes, these things are even *true*. More often, however, the so-called "modern" family farm has got one boot firmly stuck in the mud of *pre-business farming* — the old-style operation so dear to Granddad.

His was a fiercely independent operation, run harvest to harvest by a farmer who took as much of his income out of the ground as out of the "profits," usually more. His was the farm of tradition, of "unspoiled" pastoral splendor. He never heard of "return on investment." His was the descendant of the subsistence farm.

It served him very well, the conservative in us whispers, so why can't it do the same for us? In this era of "modern" farming, we still see the great influence of Granddad and his "pre-business" farm. His powerful personality is still very much with us, helping to make the "pre-business" farm almost sacred.

Farm programs by the hundreds have been geared to saving these "family" farms, whether they were sound businesses or not. There were no real measures. How could someone even think of measuring such a venerable institution?

Yet, it seems we must. "Granddad's farm" just isn't doing all that well left totally unchanged and to itself.

HISTORY MAKES LITTLE DIFFERENCE

We are assuming, you've probably noticed, that the family farm was founded by "Grandfather."

Sure, this isn't exactly true. In most cases, it was actually

Great-Granddad, or Great-Great Granddad. Sometimes it was Grandma. But for the purposes of this book, at least, we can proceed as though the farm we see today was started by the grandfather of the present owner(s) (and, possibly, Granddad's brothers).

Thus, we'll be writing as though today's owners either inherited or (more likely) bought the family farm from a pioneering "Granddad" and, maybe, some "Grand Uncles." Even though the true "founder" may be five generations removed from the present, the farm problems which developed and have been inherited fall out just as though the founder were Dad's immediate predecessor.

We should also note that calling Granddad the "founder" of the family farm plays a little fast and loose with the reality of the situation. It's unlikely that he or any of his contemporaries thought of themselves as "founding" a family farm. They were just doing what they needed to do to eat.

In those old days, Granddad and Grandma were simply homesteading a piece of ground. They were working the land to survive, and they were among the few who survived well enough to put a little aside to buy the farms of those who weren't doing so well. If you want a capsule summary of American farm history, this is it. It was the same in the North, the South, the East and the West. Only the crops, the livestock, and the accents differed.

The business Granddad and Grandma built happened to be in agriculture. Later, it would develop some unique and difficult problems simply because it was an agricultural business. But in so many senses, the family farm is simply another family business, with many of the problems that come along with ownership of family business.

Granddad was an entrepreneur, even though he might not have thought of himself that way. He went through all the survival problems every such Great American Hero goes through. He bulled his way into the future with sheer hard work, guts, and determination. Stress was his twin sister, and she led him into all of the basic characteristics of the entrepreneur —

the secrecy, the financial conservatism, the independence and the stubbornness.

And, like any business founder, by his actions he unwittingly placed little time bombs in the foundation of the farm which would begin going off much later, when the following generations became involved.

Granddad handled his affairs as though knowledge of them by anyone else would mean the end of the world. And he ruled his family with a velvet-gloved, iron hand, all the while instilling his basic thinking and management style in the next generation. His impact didn't stop with his kids, either. His values stuck, generation after generation. There are, in fact, second-, third-, and fourth-generation farmers all over the country who are working to please fathers who have been gone for more than 20 years.

They do things the way Granddad would've done them. And Granddad did them like Great-Granddad.

Should we wonder why the same problems keep appearing?

HIS EFFECTS ON DAD — AND MOM

Before we begin suggesting answers, however, we'd better understand the nature of the problems. And, to do that, we have to understand their causes. Specifically, we should try to understand the differences between the "pioneer" farm tilled by Granddad, and the semi-modern agricultural business run many years later by "Dad," his heir, and subsequent owner-managers of the farm.

"Dad" (who, in the perspective of this book, is the owner of *today's* successful family farm business), is in a much different situation from Granddad's, but he's a lot like the old guy, too.

The modern farmer has been many years at the job of taking Granddad's operation from the horse and plow of the beginning years to the mechanized and chemically enhanced operation of today, and he's done well. Yet, despite his success, this modern farmer is sensing some new problems that Granddad never knew.

But Granddad is still around. Although his heir, the "modern farmer" (Dad) realizes that his standards, his values, even his dreams aren't entirely shared by his successors and their spouses, he doesn't see the differences as fundamental. Time, he believes, time and experience, will bring them around. He doesn't do anything active about the problem, because he doesn't really believe any action is necessary (shades of Granddad).

From the point of view of his offspring, however (whom we'll refer to here as The Kids), the generational differences look fundamental, complete, critical, and seemingly unbridgeable. They try (or think they do) reasoning, pleading, arguing, cajoling, even threatening, all to no avail. They try "everything" and still Dad doesn't "change." After a while, there's nothing left to do — short of managerial assassination, a bloodless coup, or outright desertion.

Why won't Dad understand? Is he naturally stubborn? Does he enjoy watching his heirs and their spouses gnash their teeth? Surely not, but, boy, it sure looks that way to some members of the family, particularly to Dad's daughter-in-law.

Because the heir shares his basic roots with Dad, he often can see at least *some* of his father's point of view. But almost as often, his wife (Dad's daughter-in-law) sees his "open-mindedness" as more of a handicap than wisdom. She doesn't have his "perspective." Instead, she keeps wondering, and asking, "Why?"

Dad's iron-studded, oaken fence across the road to the future is generally very difficult for her to accept, much less deal with. What makes things worse is his failure to even see the wall he's built. He loves his kids. He's not trying to be a bad guy. He's just too busy and has to keep blinders on to survive. It's not that he discounts the problems of others. He can't do anything about them, like the weather, so the best thing is to ignore them.

Dad wonders, instead, what all the fuss and complaining is about. As far as he's concerned, the only barrier to everything working out the way it should is The Kid's slow and painful progress, and his wife's "uncooperative" nature. *That's* why they can't talk the way they should. *That's* why it's so hard to agree on things.

From Dad's point of view, "succession" is progressing well enough around the farm — more slowly than he wants, probably, but progressing. His heir is learning. With all the help available — FFA, 4-H, the extension agents, etc. — he couldn't help but learn. The problem, and there is one, is The Kid's failure to understand simple things like the real world, and life, and what farming is *really* all about.

The kid's lack of understanding has driven him nuts almost from the beginning. Dad's always been buried in problems. His eyebrows have been singed over and over again by the brush fires he's fought every day, his boots thick with operational "manure." He built a successful farm despite all the odds against him, then found himself spending much of his time trying to hold it all together in the face of financial worries and a changing world. Little wonder he's now bothered by an heir who just doesn't have the "spark."

(We can wonder about "spark." What is it? What does it mean not to have it? One answer comes from something a successor's mom once said to us: *"Our son bought a Corvette instead of land. Is this a difference in personality? Temperament? The times? Or maybe my husband didn't take the time to coach him on how to successfully carry on the family farm. Maybe our son's delayed maturity could be due to growing up in too 'cushy' an environment without enough healthy deprivation . . ."* Maybe. And maybe it could also be a sign of uncertainty — about the future, about the farm, even about Dad's intentions.)

Dad doesn't need problems from his heir. What he needs most of all is help.

But what does he get from The Kid? Questions, more questions, and, worst of all, suggestions on how to change the farm to make it "grow."

In the face of this, his objective becomes primarily to teach The Kid, and any of his other children who will listen, the "truth" about farming (a lot of which came from Granddad). This he does. With force and conviction — and more angry oaths than constructive suggestions.

The "lessons" learned will stay with the farm far into the future.

THE BASIC VALUES ARE FORMED — AND FOLLOWED

Granddad's farm, like any new business, started with next to nothing. There was little cash in the cash box. There was hardly any balance in the "balance sheet." There wasn't much of anything, in fact, other than hard work, worry, long hours, and anxiety for the future.

Granddad hadn't a lot of certainty that the harvest would come in, or that his crop would bring a reasonable price, or that he'd be able to pay the loan when it came due. His only real advantage over his in-town cousins was that he knew, at least, where the next meal was coming from. Thus was the family farm trend-line set, and thus would it be picked up after him, generation after generation, by his heirs.

This was the time that Granddad (and, remember, his sons and their sons take Granddad's style to heart as their own) picked up the most obvious characteristic of his evolving personality: *secrecy*. The farmer tells nobody nuttin', nuttin' of any substance, anyway. You ask him how much fertilizer he's using and he'll want to know why you're poking around in his business.

Is this because tilling the ground makes one congenitally secretive? Nope. It's just that there's no reason for anyone to know how tough things are. It's bad enough that *he* knows. In solitary, courageous splendor, he lies, night after night in a pool of cold sweat. He has his nightly three-a.m "blink" sessions, wide awake, staring at the bedroom ceiling, wondering how he's going to get through the season.

Often, the same ceiling is stared at, in turn, by many generations of family farmers, and, today, we can safely assume it's Dad who's lying in Granddad's place. Next to this Great American Agricultural Hero lies Mom. She's wide awake, too, but her eyes are closed. She doesn't want him to know that she knows that he's scared half to death. He's protecting her, but what doesn't she know already? She saw the hailstorm in July. The dry August. The heavy rains around harvest time. She recognizes cases of bloody scours when she sees them, and thin farm prices when she reads about them.

But he's protecting her.

And, in the process, he's cutting out one of his best allies.

Oh, sure, they work together night and day. Nobody on a struggling farm can sit around and just watch things happen, but they each have their own place in the operation. Dad is very firmly out there in the fields, in the barn, and hovering anxiously over his dairy herd. Those things are for her to worry about, too, of course, but he doesn't like to talk about it. So they worry separate — and different.

To be sure, if Dad and Mom were alone on the farm, raised enough for themselves, then sold the place to land developers in their retirement years, it wouldn't matter much what Dad did managing the farm. It wouldn't matter to future generations, at least.

But just like Granddad, his progeny, Mom and Dad, were not alone. Not for long. Even though they worked from dawn to dusk (and later), there were those cold winter nights, too, when the big quilt felt awfully cozy. Dad and Mom, like their parents, managed with everything else they were doing to, somehow, have offspring. Their kids steadily filled up the house.

Actually, it was only with the arrival of Dad's kids that his approach to farming began to take on immortal overtones. Oh, the kids didn't really understand what was going on. Not at first. They were five, six, 10, just kids (and everyone knows no kid becomes conscious of his or her surroundings until about age 30 or so). No, they didn't understand the specifics, but they did see that Daddy was resigned to some distant (and not all that friendly) fate. They had their noses rubbed in what he did every day, but they didn't really understand why he did it at all if it was that "tough." Too bad they didn't get the good side of the story, too, but Dad didn't think that was important in the scheme of things.

He complained about the weather. He grumbled about the bankers. He bemoaned the price of fertilizer and feed. He worried about the cost of equipment and, ultimately, was devastated by the price of corn. He fussed about weeds and he fumed about weevils and borers and grubs.

And in almost the same breath, he would periodically take The Kid, and maybe some of his brothers, out to the west pasture at sunset and tell them about how, someday, the farm would all be theirs.

This is called "early management training" on the family farm.

THE "GROWTH" YEARS

Those were the early years. Eventually, though, things got better for Dad, and survival eventually faded as a primary concern.

We're discussing the winners here, remember, the farmers who managed to get far enough ahead to expand when their neighbors failed. Eventually, the family homestead, with success, could safely begin to call itself a "family farm."

Dad began to see a little cash in the cash box and some balance in the bank book. There'd been a few good years, he learned something more about farming, and he'd picked up some help — particularly the kids. He steadily increased his stature in the county, the co-op, and in town. He became a pillar of the community.

So, now, couldn't we expect him to shed his cloak of secrecy? After all, there's nothing bad to hide anymore, not even from Mom.

Well, yes, there was no longer a need to cover up, but there were many things people wouldn't have understood all that well. And, besides, by then Dad had had a few years to discover this new partner of his, Old Uncle Sam. What people wouldn't understand was that his good years were only offsetting the bad years to come. If he told them that things were fine, they would get the wrong picture of how things really were.

He maybe didn't play all the tax games that the in-town business owner took for granted as a part of life, but he did think a lot about the Keogh's and the IRA's and all of the more obvious ways to salt money away for the bad years (which he knew from experience were coming). He was anything but cocky, so he saw no reason to boast.

Which, to him, was saying anything to anybody about anything.

He continued to tell nobody nuttin', keeping it all from the bank, from the suppliers, from Mom and from the Kids. The farm was making money. He was running the farm. And everything important there was to know about running that farm was locked up securely in his head.

Everybody else, even the kids, was "The Help." He loved them. He took care of them. They just didn't need to know.

THE KID'S EARLY "TRAINING"

There would be no problem with this secretive dictatorship if all we were discussing was an agricultural hobby staffed with hired help. But by the point most family farms begin to taste some success, the next generation of heirs, The Kids, are at work in relatively significant jobs, not just chores.

The Kid knows what he's doing, too, with all his training from the land grant college, the 4-H, the FFA. He's a good farmer. What he doesn't get from Dad is much information on the business side of farming — for one reason, because Dad isn't all that sure, himself, of the off-farm, real-world business side of things.

The Kid, for our purposes, is the first heir to a modern "family farm." As such, he represents the seed corn of the future. Without him, the continuity of the family farm is in doubt.

Given this, we would assume that Dad has raised and trained him to be a farm manager with as much care as he raised him to be a farmer. Except we'd be wrong. In far too many family farms, the process of "successor training" is so misguided, so poorly thought through, and so poisonous to the successful growth of the heirs being trained, that the primary effect is to throw barbed coils of confusion and misinformation in their paths.

This isn't to say they won't be successful — enough of them are, in spite of their experiences, to impress us with the strength and resiliency of the human spirit — but this educational failure makes life much tougher than it has to be, and unfairly diminishes the chances for success.

To understand why, we need to take a closer look at this process called "growing up on the farm."

Chapter 4
GROWING UP ON THE FARM

The farm "Kid" begins his education long before anybody, including Dad, ever imagines. It begins long before even
the first chore. It begins almost at birth.

But nobody knows.

Dad, for his part, went on with his work just as before.
If anything, he noticed the kids only because they didn't do their
chores or because they got in the way or into danger. About the
best way to describe Dad's attitude toward his children is a lov-
ing lack of awareness. He's too busy.

This is a lack of awareness, however, that his kids don't
share. As soon as consciousness dawns, definitely long before
the so-called "age of reason," Dad's heirs become very aware,
indeed, of the family farm. In their early years, the kids soak
up their environment like sponges. They watch, and they absorb what they see without much critical judgment. They might
have little basis for understanding and comparison — but they
make comparisons nevertheless, and they do think they understand.

Dad and Mom might not be discussing farm matters a lot with their children, but that doesn't mean the kids aren't noticing the farm. Quietly, in their own attentive way, they're getting their elementary farm management education.

Unfortunately, it's not a very good one, because they are effectively forced to train themselves.

Dad, meanwhile, is busily playing the hero (and a little bit of the martyr). Even this wouldn't be so bad if he just kept it consistent. But his successes are shot through with worries. His highs are so high and his lows so low that the confused signals he gives off baffle everyone around him. When the weather is good and prices are high, he rightly accepts all the praise and glory. When the harvest is bad or prices hit bottom, there's nobody to blame but himself. Those are violent swings and the effect on him is disorienting.

Dad's battle is intense and unrelenting. He has no personal foxhole to dive into, no place to rest. Exhaustion takes its toll, but (he's a hero, remember) he hides all of this from his family. At least, he *tries*. Generally, he fails.

He says very little to Mom (he doesn't want her to worry), but, of course, she knows. She knows better than he, in fact, because she's not distorting reality through a dream — not as much as he is. So Mom's worried, too.

And so are the kids. They may not understand, but they miss little of what's going on.

What *is* going on? Well, it's hard for the kids to know. Dad's his silent, autocratic self, and Mom suffers in silence. Usually. Sometimes, though, they have some intense "discussions." The kids hear. They don't know what it's specifically all about, but they do suspect it has something to do with "The Farm."

Around the corner, tucked away in their rooms, the heirs are wondering and imagining about this vague frustration in their lives. As they grow up in it, they don't usually learn a lot more about the real problems, only that those city folk are profiting at the farmer's expense. They just know that farming must be very difficult — and that it's going to be their job someday to survive it, too.

LEARNING THE ROPES: FARMING OR MANAGEMENT?

Perhaps, it would be best if Dad's heirs didn't step into management of the family farm until The Chief was ready to let loose of *some* control. Perhaps they should go off to learn farm management somewhere else — or in their own operation.

Some experts would even consider this the ideal approach.

But we're realistic enough to know that a majority of farm heirs work immediately, and without significant break other than for education, on the family farm.

This is the fact.

But acceptance doesn't mean we shouldn't make the best of the situation. If they can't get their management training off the farm, then we'd better make sure they get it on the farm. We'd better be sure they're starting with a *real* job.

Of course, you say. Easy, you say. There are all sorts of real jobs around the place. But are there? If it's so simple, why are the kinds of jobs offered so often the last consideration when hiring farm heirs?

Too often, the major considerations are the heir's age and readiness for work — which are seldom, if ever, in sync with the need of the farm for a manager. Farm employment, for heirs at least, is more based on the laws of puberty than the laws of economics.

In reality, the hiring of family business heirs never really happens. "Working" is what they've always been doing, only one day the laws of economics kick in: *"Since we feed them anyway, they might as well earn their keep."* This comes almost as a surprise, as though nobody knew the young son or daughter was actually getting older. Plan for their coming of age? Heaven forbid. We'll just make their allowance deductible:

> *"They gotta learn to farm, so they might as well get started."*

Or:

> *"This way he won't have to waste his time learning*

about somebody else's farm. The only farm he needs to know is OURS."

Or:

"We just plain need the help . . . and right now."

HIRING THE UNDER-QUALIFIED

Let's take these one at a time, since they cover most of the rationalizations for hiring farm heirs without outside experience.

1) **The "Might As Well Get To It" Argument.** This, given the reality of the situation, is fundamentally a self-delusion. On the farm, The Kid is trained to be a good worker, not usually taught how to manage or how to make decisions. If, in fact, the job available on the family farm were a *real* job — which we define as a job that carries an appropriate level of *management* responsibility and maybe even some training in the realities of running a farm — it might be the best choice.

But is it?

Nope.

Sure, it's a good thing to learn to work, but if all The Kid does while in training is feed hogs or grind corn, that's all he'll ever learn to do. Mostly Dad raises great workers, not great farmers.

As the sons of one farm owner we knew lamented after Dad died:

"Dad taught us how to farm, but he didn't bother teaching us how to keep the books."

And the other side of this coin is the fact that the farm is usually as unprepared for the heir as he is for the farm. Dad believes he's getting The Kid ready to take it over some day, so the sooner he starts, the better, but "start" at what? Dad doesn't really know.

Nor does he know that, deep down, he has little intention of letting it go anyway.

The most unfortunate part of the whole situation is that the The Kid (the heir, remember), in his innocence, accepts Dad's "Someday, it'll all be yours" as reality, too. For one thing, he wants to believe it. For another, he's too confused about how to go from being a worker to becoming a farmer to question much of anything, including the reality of his job.

Dad plays the game well, too. So do the hired hands (who are they to buck The Boss?). On the surface, everything looks like non-fiction, but underneath, where it really counts, the farm heir is skipping down that yellow brick road to Oz, with little real prospect of getting anything — other than a farm hand's wages.

There's no credibility at the outset and, therefore, no respect. As the student begins making the inevitable mistakes, the road to disillusionment (The Kid's) and disappointment (Dad's) is direct and downhill.

In fact, the key to developing a farm owner-manager is not to give him a job, but a *real* job that prepares him for *management* responsibility (and then increases that responsibility judiciously) — something often forgotten on the family farm. The acid test is to ask the question "Are we training a family farmer, or are we assuming we have one and just waiting for him to show himself?"

Make-work jobs on the fringes — no matter how much everybody wants to believe they're "needed" — are no answer either. The under-employment rate among family farm heirs is staggeringly high and universally unrecognized. It's unemployment with a paycheck, but it's unemployment nevertheless. The Kid may even go to the bank with Dad, but he's never asked for his opinion, not about anything important.

It would be almost impossible even for an experienced non-family professional farmer to survive a job like this. Because there's seldom any planning, any definition, or any agreement on what the objectives are, a farm manager put into this sort of job is forced to fly blind through a fog, hoping for a break. Eventually, he runs smack into Old North Forty, himself, and the makeshift airlift is over. At least an outsider can learn and leave, chastened but wiser — as many thousands have.

But the farm heir is *family*. "Sure, it's his fault it didn't work out, but we'll give him another chance." For what? To fail, of course.

It's a neat dilemma. To stay on the farm means an uphill battle for credibility and responsibility, weighed down by mounting frustration. To leave means accepting defeat, antagonizing the family, and going off to farm on your own with less efficiency, and even less confidence than before.

The only cure for this creeping paralysis is a real job, with real responsibilities, real performance standards, and objective evaluation. The farm heir, after all, shouldn't be learning to be an employee. He's supposedly learning to be an owner, with all the headaches and risks that unique position carries with it. He needs real management training and real communication, driven by real acceptance of his "need to know" for the future.

And to learn to be an owner, he has to *experience* ownership. Oh, he has his own form of three a.m. "blink" sessions — he and his wife — but they aren't about how to survive. They're about how Dad "won't let me decide anything" or about how "he won't even tell me anything."

Frustration runs high. We should wonder why The Kid goes off and milks for somebody else. A client of ours had a neighbor whose son, a National Merit Scholar with a four-year university education, left the family farm "without so much as a talk with the folks."

2) **The "Let's Get to It" Argument**. For many farm families, it's a foregone conclusion that time spent working on another farm or for somebody else is time spent learning things that won't be much help running the family farm. After all, "our farm is different."

What most farm owners and heirs fail to consider, though, is that tomorrow's family farm is going to be different, too. Different from today's. Today's farmers are fighting today's battles — a valid and essential activity. But the heir is intended as tomorrow's farm manager and he should be preparing to win tomorrow's agricultural war. He can't do that very efficiently in today's trenches.

An heir with an entry level "management" job on the family farm too often isn't learning how to manage. He's learning farming *history*. He learns to keep quiet, to listen, to watch, and *to stay out of the way*. During this period, he hears (and hears again) the war stories and gets "educated" as to how this farm has held together over the years. He learns there are sacred rituals and secret understandings that bind the older operators together. And that's about it.

To venture a question, even with proper humility, is to risk a plague of locusts and a size 14 boot.

Does Dad teach? Nope. He *demonstrates*. The heir hasn't been around long enough to understand the subtleties and finer points. He's not initiated, so he can't join the ceremonies — and if (Heaven forbid) he is a *she*, the poor heir can barely expect to witness them. (In fact, the farmer's daughter is usually taken more seriously in jokes than in discussions about owning and managing the farm. About the only time *she* exists is if there is no *he*.)

The only route left is explanation, which is highly unlikely. Dad, his partners, and the older employees never really had to think through what they do. Their management "style" evolved through a continuing process of mistakes, flurries of desperate activity, and survival. Agricultural training under these conditions, when it exists at all, is little more than a series of loosely connected "just so" stories. "That, youngster, is the way we've always done it."

The problems aren't in learning farming techniques. The agricultural industry, perhaps more than any other, has worked out fine programs for training young people to understand the techniques of farming. No, the problems lay in learning ownership and management, the handling of funds, the subtleties of marketing, financing production, that sort of thing.

The central sorts of things.

At least, working off-farm, in an agribusiness or non-farm company, the heir is more likely to get a real job and the chance to learn and make mistakes in action, to form management theories and develop a business philosophy based on something more concrete than legend and fraternal mysteries. Typically, this doesn't happen working on any farm, his family's or somebody else's. But if the heir is going to begin on the family farm, this sort of opportunity has to be available to him.

The "real" farm job is crucially important — making sure he gets it is a dual responsibility, his and Dad's.

3) **The "We Need Him Now" Argument**. As with any of these arguments, this one can be valid, particularly since most family farms can't afford to hire competent, non-family employees. The smaller and younger the farm involved, the more likely the heir *will* be needed — as cheap (wage-wise) management. Unfortunately, we get what we pay for. At least, when there's a lot of work and nobody available to do it, the heir's job will be real.

Such timing is a matter of judgment, but one hard question must be asked. If the heir is brought in today to fill a gaping hole in our labor force, what price will we have to pay in cutting short his or her management training for the future? Will the heir just get trapped by today's brush fires? Is that good for the farm?

Questions like this can't be answered with certainty, but we can sense the right road to take. Family farm heirs are potential owner-managers of *real* farms with *real* management needs. Whatever training they get, whether it's on or off the farm, should, itself, be *real* — and, to the extent it's possible, the best available.

WHEN THE GENERATIONS DISAGREE

Real training and real experience are the first steps in managing the development of our heirs. The next step is understanding and finding ways to handle the inevitable disagreements.

First off, we've got to understand what causes the disagreements. Disagreements between generations on family farms can be about facts — farming techniques, the need for marketing — but they can also be about personal opinions — the future, acceptable risk levels, the best way to behave — (which the theorists like to call "values").

Many of the problems between Dad and The Kid, indeed, between almost any generations in family farms come about because of the inability to know what sort of disagreement is in progress.

Carrying this thought further, it's safe to say that "generations" don't disagree about matters of fact. Not usually. Instead, they disagree about opinions or personal values, but they *think* and *act* as though facts are at issue. This fundamental confusion is the most common reason why so many of the successor's "new ideas" meet with "resistance" from The Old Man.

It's an unfortunate fact of experience that disagreements between Dad and his heirs tend to escalate to confrontation. Even worse can be the "discussions" that go on among siblings on a second-generation farm (or cousins in the third generation).

Most people can differ reasonably on matters of fact. Matters of personal needs and desires — values — usually prove to be tough, however, and fundamental. When the difference isn't even recognized — as too often it isn't — reaching consensus becomes almost impossible.

Farm management issues are heavily loaded with many different values components, but our experience has underlined four major categories of disagreement:

1) **Business Goals.**

How one approaches management decisions on a farm can vary greatly depending on what one expects for and from that farm.

A farm owner wanting to build an agricultural empire is going to approach decisions quite differently from someone who is only running a profitable hobby. A commitment to growth is quite different from a commitment to profit or cash flow, and the two can quite often be incompatible — at least in the short term.

And these are only two examples from a list of possible goals. What about selling land, going into retail sales, non-farm income . . .?

2) **Personal Goals.**

On family farms, the desire some people have for income stability and security often flies in the face of others' desires for income growth and challenge. In many senses, these are incompatible values — yet neither is right or wrong. It's impossible to "prove" one over the other as the desirable way to go, yet many arguments over business decisions are really (and unconsciously, in so many cases) disagreements over growth versus stability.

3) **Acceptable Level of Risk.**

At a consulting session, we once asked an heir and his father to estimate the maximum amount of money their operation could afford to lose on a new venture. The owner said they couldn't afford to lose a cent, while his son estimated a quarter of a million dollars!

This wasn't only a disagreement over dollars. It was a disagreement that arose from their different business and personal goals. A farm owner in his 60's sees much less long-term benefit in risk-taking than he did 10 or more years ago in his 50's. In his 40's he was much more comfortable with risk, and in his 20's or 30's, it was probably his ultimate challenge. It might be that the successor is only expressing an attitude the owner, himself, held 20 or so years ago.

But Dad doesn't hold it now, and he's not likely to, ever again.

4) **The Keys to Farm Success.**

Family farms succeed for many reasons. Some make it on innovation. Others on brilliant crop or livestock or financial management. In some cases, marketing is a major factor, while others depend on low cost and efficient production. These are matters of life cycle, crop/livestock mix, and markets — but they're also matters of personal strengths and preferences.

A farm run by an agricultural wizard tends to make it on innovation and skill more than any other factor. A farm run by a brilliant marketer will tend to base a lot of its success on numbers. Facts and the past say one way is better than another in a given company, which is fine — until the next generation moves in.

Farm heirs walk onto operations built on the strengths and preferences of somebody else (Dad), and agreement to continue focusing in this direction depends on whether The Boss and the successor share the same specific talent genes.

That likelihood, of course, is very small.

These are matters of management style, personal objectives, and fundamental beliefs. They can't be proved or disproved. Instead, they must be thoroughly explored, together, by all key managers on family farms as a necessary beginning to work through conflict and resistance. Family farm operators must, in short, quit the fruitless debates and concentrate on understanding their values differences.

What makes Dad seem like an irresistible force *and* an immovable object is his inability to accept his heir's "facts" as convincing arguments. What the successor sees as a necessary (if hopeless) restatement of the realities of a situation, Dad sees as inexperience and an inability to listen to common sense. Both believe they are pushing facts, when, in actuality, both are standing firm on opposing values.

And neither understands what's happening.

There is no quick fix, no rope bridge that can be thrown in an instant over the "generation gap." Solving values differences on the family farm is a process, and it takes time, commitment, and mutual understanding. Sure, specific disagreements can be solved on the spot, as they usually are, by Dad's tie-breaker, but that's about as viable a long-term solution to disagreement as martial law is to political dissent.

Nobody is really immovable. No idea is really irresistible. It just seems that way some times. It's entirely possible, of course, that the values of the successors and The Boss, or the goals of the cousins or the spouses won't agree. But they can be helped to converge over time. They almost surely will if the process is honestly followed, some objective moderation is brought in, and reality is allowed to temper convictions.

Whatever is done, however, decisions must be made. Settling for conflict, frustration, or disappointment has no place on a family farm — not, at least, on one which everyone agrees should survive and grow.

There's just too much to do . . . and too much to lose.

Chapter 5
DAD AND HIS PROBLEMS

Granddad is followed on the farm by his heir, a person or group of persons whom we will call "The Modern Farmer" or, simply, "Dad."

This "succession" happens with varying success in every family farm that isn't sold or liquidated by Granddad, and succession comes to Dad both as a great relief and a whole new set of problems.

Dad's finally on his own — on his own, that is, if you ignore his brother, sometimes a cousin or two, and his sister with a piece of the farm who lives in town, and the kids roaming around the place. He's building the operation, making his own success (in their minds, of course, with their considerable help and advice).

This is what all the pain and patience was for, yet at the top of his career he finds some bitter winds taking the joy out of the beautiful view. Dad, in short, finds that success hasn't solved all of his problems. It solved some, of course, but it brought many others, problems and dilemmas that Granddad never had:

1) *Dad faces sons with even bigger ideas than the ideas he had.*

This is only natural. After all, the farm is bigger. There's more money involved. Farming is one heck of a lot more technical and complicated than ever before, with every decision based more and more on the numbers. Why should he expect his young Turks to have anything but wider (and wilder) ideas about the future?

He had some grand schemes himself during the days he wrestled with Granddad, sure, but his dreams never approached the scope, size, and sheer audacity of what his sons are coming up with. At least his mistakes Granddad could afford.

But what his offspring are pushing for is something else entirely. The risks are so much greater, and who's to say they can even pull it off? He knows he doesn't want to gamble, so . . .

2) *Dad must, somehow, educate his heirs beyond the old wisdoms of farming.*

If he's ever going to let them handle a significant part of the operation, they've got to know a lot more than even he can teach them. Heck, he can't even teach himself everything he needs to know to run the operation. To tell the truth, he doesn't really know what needs to be learned, or how to get it learned, or who to teach it to, or when, so he's waiting, hoping he'll figure something out.

Then, if he doesn't have any (or even enough) children to fill his needs for successor-managers . . .

3) *Dad may have to find ways to attract, develop and work with non-family successors, maybe even (you gotta be kidding!) his son-in-law.*

It's not unusual for a farm owner to find himself or herself with no family heirs. Sometimes this is simply because he lacks heirs. But it's also possible the children he has aren't interested in farming, or that he hasn't enough time to wait for sons or daughters to get ready. So, on top of all his other problems, he's got to go outside the family for key managers.

This is tough on Old Dad. Blood is blood and strangers are strangers. Yet, he knows he has to do something, so he hires a non-family successor and goes to work "grooming" him for the job.

But whether the successor is a family heir or a non-family key employee, the grooming he gets is generally haphazard and usually very slow. Dad's heirs, whether or not they're related to him, eventually rebel at the lack of movement. They get frustrated. Sometimes they get angry. They're joined in this by all the minority owners.

Dad, of course, has no retirement plan to speak of. How could he? The profits are slim, and those fancy Keogh Plans, IRA's, and so forth are only recent developments. Fact is, the farm itself remains the primary security of the farm owner and his wife. Someone has to continue to run the farm in a way that provides enough income . . . no, an endless stream of security for Mom and Dad. With that as a prospect, how can he leave?

He holds on, hoping for the best, and says very little to the successors. After all, they're the problem. And they can't really talk to Dad about their frustrations since "he's the problem," so they go home and grumble to their spouses.

Here come more problems for the farm, as we note below.

The minority owners? Well, they just wonder what's going on. In short . . .

4) *Dad faces a set of increasingly restless share-holders, co-owners, partners, relatives and in-laws.*

For one thing (since most farm heirs today are male, although that's changing, too), he faces problems with his daughter-in-law. Her spouse has cast his lot (and, therefore, hers) with his family's farm, yet all she seems to see is frustration and delay, without any of the benefits she *thinks* she's been promised over the years. She wants and needs reassurance and communication, but she can't get that from Dad.

Since the successor's grumbling is just about the only picture of the family farm that Dad's daughter-in-law is likely to get, *she* becomes one of the revolutionary leaders. More and more daughters-in-law are employed off the farm in careers of their own. They have to be to generate the extra income most farm families need. But this means that Dad's daughters-in-law are less and less likely to be cut from the same cloth that Mom was. They are a lot less likely to understand the business of farming and, therefore, a lot less understanding of Dad.

But she's not the only problem in his extended agricultural family. He may have a brother who's ill and wants to be bought out, or a partner who's not carrying his share, or a sister in Santa Fe who owns half the operation and has a husband with crazy ideas.

All these people circle around him, pushing, nagging, requesting, suggesting, criticizing. And where does he go? Who does he talk to? Well . . .

5) *Dad must find a way to begin communicating with Mom, the silent ally he's been "protecting"*

all these years, because that's what she's begin-
ning to demand.

She probably understands the problems of
farming pretty well, because she's been so involved over the years. Often, she's the family farm
"dragon" keeping the books and protecting the
family "jewels." She shares a lot of Dad's dreams
and a lot of his frustrations, but she shares them
from a different point of view.

She wants to know more about what he's
thinking, and she wants him to listen better to what
she's thinking. Mom has learned a lot over the
years. She was once a farm owner's daughter-in-
law herself. She's not ready now to take the passive role her mother-in-law did. And even if she
were ready, she has children involved, and her
children's spouses, all of whom find in her a ready
ear about their problems. Somebody has to in-
tercede, to referee, to mediate, and she seems to
be it.

The kids have a right to be concerned, she
knows, and they need to communicate with Dad.
But the operation is also getting to be too much
for him. The more she tries to talk about the problems, the more impatient and closed he becomes.

You can't go on forever, she tells him. It's
time to do something. He hears. He knows.
But . . .

6) *Dad must pass down a significant business —*
not "just a farm" — to his heirs, and the personal
concerns and financial complexities of doing that
seem overwhelming.

As if he didn't have enough trouble trying
to survive and to get the kids to take some "responsibility" for things (responsibility for grinding
the corn, however, not making business deci-

sions). Now he has to find some method for passing the farm down to the next generation, while he satisfies all the present owners, including himself.

It didn't seem to be so hard when he bought it from Granddad. It didn't cost anything then compared to now, and there weren't all those taxes. He wants them to buy it just the way he did because that's the right way to do it, but every time he looks into it, the numbers just don't work out.

Now, with all the changes and all the people involved, he has to find a way to design his estate that preserves his security, that doesn't give them too much too soon, that's fair to the other owners and off-farm heirs, and that manages to keep the whole thing out of Uncle Sam's hands.

Fortunately, other than the issues above, Dad doesn't have any problems to speak of. Except, of course, high interest rates, bankers who are friends but increasingly powerless to help him, lousy prices and bad weather. Fortunately . . .

We wonder why he lies awake in three a.m. "blink" sessions?

He looks in that bathroom mirror at four in the morning and says to himself, "This situation is getting out of control." When Grandpa was around, it was simply his place, but now I'm in business with my brother, and some of the land is owned by Sister Kate in Des Moines (who, unfortunately, married that lawyer!). The kids have been to college and now they're talking about a lot of things that make me real uncomfortable. I'm in with the bank more than I ever thought I would be.

This whole thing depends on my body, and everybody's after me to do something.

Dad is a successful farm owner. He is also a pressured husband, a disappointed teacher, a frightened, aging male, and a confused manager. He wants things to be the way they've always been. He feels a responsibility for that. But the world has changed so much . . .

He's at the top of his world, yet he's tired, harassed, confused about what to do next, and has nobody to ask for advice or help.

This is the other side of what it means to own a successful family farm.

THE SONS WITH BIG IDEAS

My Lord, Dad sighs in the quiet of his bedroom late at night, don't they understand how complex this whole thing is? What I need is a little help fighting off the daily wolf that shows up with the rising sun. That's what needs doing. That's problem enough as far as he's concerned. He only wants to be able to take a couple of weeks off now and then, but the people around him can't stand in for him. They only know how to grind corn (because that's all he's managed to teach them).

So what kind of help does he get? He gets ideas and suggestions from heirs who have, maybe, a little too much education and not enough common sense. All they seem to want to do is raise the level of risk without offering benefits that meet his standards. He learned many years ago that change means work, lots of it, and more money than he's ready to borrow. He already has more debt than he wants to handle.

In Dad's mind, caution is justified. In The Kids' minds, that caution is more a dead hand on the controls than anything else. Just as Dad doesn't understand their level of frustration, they don't understand his loneliness and insecurity.

So they handle their campaign for more responsibility with all the subtlety of a bull moose in mating season. A lot of blame for stagnation is dumped in Dad's lap, but he doesn't deserve all of it. Some, yes, but a lot of the problem the Kid brings on himself.

The Kid tends to be his own worst enemy. First, it's tough to evaluate your own ideas when you're young and short on experience. It's tougher yet to believe there could be anything wrong with them. Second, it's all too easy to present a great idea in a manner almost guaranteed to result in rejection.

The usual procedure is for The Kid to hatch a bright idea

in a frustrated search for something interesting and challenging to grab onto. Then he runs it by his spouse, with a few "eure-kas!" She, of course, has even less experience than he does — but she has the greater wisdom to know he needs support, en-couragement and advice. So they discuss the idea.

Only after she is also deeply involved and identified with the idea does he get around to *suggesting* it to Dad. Notice we're talking here about a suggestion, not a proposal to do something. Instead of "I want to . . . , and here's how . . . ," Dad's son says, "I think *we* should . . . " It's such a brilliant idea, surely Dad will see its value immediately and praise his heir for coming up with such a brilliant thought.

But what response does The Kid get. Usually none. If there is an answer, it's usually something on the order of "Good idea . . . let's talk about it sometime." Which means, of course, at Dad's convenience, which will be seldom if ever. He was too busy this week. Maybe next month after the plowing's done. Or at the fair in July . . .

To tell the truth, Dad doesn't want to talk about The Kid's idea at all. He hasn't the time — and even if he did, what would be the point? There's no time or money for follow-through any-way. He's learned one thing in all his years on the farm: If it ain't broke, don't fix it.

The problem is, as most successful farmers know from experience, there's no shortage of new ideas. This is true, in general, in business all across the globe. What *is* in short supply is action, turning ideas into operating profit.

The successful family farm is generally stuck reacting to events rather than planning the future, precisely because there is so much to do. Important factors that in-town business owners take for granted — particularly prices and costs — are out of the farmer's control. The real problem, in Dad's eyes, is getting the day-to-day work done so we can survive.

If a new idea is going to have any value, the background work and the planning have to be done by somebody — and there's nobody to spare. Nobody, that is, from Dad's point of view. The heir thinks he's available (and probably is), but he never gets around to really volunteering. That would require a long, direct flight through Dad's negative experience and unconscious flak, a mighty unpleasant prospect, one that's too easily put off. Thus, The Kid presents an "idea" instead of a proposal. It's really a trial balloon, which after some experience he fully expects Dad to shoot down.

The big problem with the way the idea is presented is the word "we." The first and most active reaction Dad has to this kind of suggestion is to raise a jaded eyebrow to that heavily loaded word. We, who?

The "we" might be The Kid's way of bringing Dad into "owning" the problem, but Dad is likely to read it as simply "you do it, Dad."

So Dad just sets it aside as too much trouble. Pigheadedness, his son will call it. Stubbornness. Hardening of the ambitions. Conservatism. There are a lot of phrases for this resistance from the power structure. But words are no help when the heir comes home mumbling about roadblocks to Dad's daughter-in-law. What she has to say about it all couldn't even be written into a rock song.

Thus does Dad get the reputation of being a barnacle on the rump of progress.

It's a reputation generally undeserved. Even the heirs would have to admit they've never known Dad to object to a sound new idea, supported by evidence that it would expand the business, increase revenue or strengthen profits. The problem lies squarely wedged in that yawning crack between the "good idea" and the "successful project."

Every venture begins with the intuitive leap, the "Idea," but that idea is only raw material. Agricultural ventures aren't artistic creations composed in inspired solitude in a hay loft in mid-October. They are intimately involved in the changing world around them — and so must be their creators. Managers of family farms — indeed, of businesses in general — manage *economic* creativity, which carries as one of its central premises the requirement that the creator also be a *doer*. Ideas are useless in the economic world unless they have positive results.

New ideas without sensible implementation plans and reasonable budgets are worse than useless, in fact, because they too often waste precious and limited funds, man-hours, and resources.

Coming up with an idea is only the first step in the process of business development. The major responsibility is the pursuit of that idea into economic viability. Ideas are as common as earthworms in loose soil. It's making an idea workable that turns it into an IDEA.

Dad's problem with his heirs often boils down to his difficulty "educating" them to this simple fact.

FUTURE FARMERS/BUSINESS MANAGERS

For the first time in all the many generations that have passed across the land, education is becoming an issue. Granddad saw farming as something one did to live. Dad looked on it as a way of life and a living. But now, suddenly, it has become a business. And running a business takes specialized knowledge.

Nobody would claim there's a shortage of places that teach the technical skills of agriculture. Nor have young farmers failed to take advantage of those resources. Iowa State University did a study of 2,293 Iowa families in 1983 and found that 58% of farm youth have post-high school educations. This compared with 33% of their parents. Four-year college degrees have been earned by 25% of these young people. Truth is, today's farm heir is the best educated in history — in the science of agriculture.

The need for this kind of training is clear to Dad, and it's clear to his heirs. So, usually, the farm heir is well-trained in farming. But if the modern farmer is being forced more and more into managing his operation like a business, shouldn't business education also be part of the training of farm successors?

"More and more, successful farmers are those who coordinate their production plans with financing and marketing plans in a closely inte-

grated management system. In effect, they are not farmers, but businessmen whose business is farming."[1]

In the past, more farmers made their money on land appreciation than in crop production, but the trend today is in a different direction. Dad knows this. He can see it as well as any in-town financial expert. But deciding what to do about it is another question altogether.

Clearly, the future of the farm will be managed by the heirs, not by Dad, and even though he must steadily increase his knowledge of finance and marketing, he's really not the manager with the greatest need to know. The successor-managers need the training much more than Dad does. Yet, what training do the heirs get? Much the same as Dad got under Granddad's wing.

At least for Dad, Granddad's teachings were somewhat relevant for his future — for a while. But for today's farm heirs, those same lessons mean learning farm management *history* more than anything else.

History won't help all that much. Not any more. Not in the future the American farm is facing. We blame all kinds of external factors for the problems we have — high interest rates and low commodity prices, in particular — but if these were the true problems, every farm operation would be in trouble. But not everyone is. No, the problems of survival on the family farm, just as in the in-town family business, exist internally in the management practices of the owners.

> " . . . *if I were to isolate one common variable, it's clearly inadequate financial management and accounting. It stems from the fact that of all the businesses in America, only agriculture has been permitted to operate outside of generally accepted accounting and business principles.*"[2]

Training is a question of time and resources, of course.

Since the operation needs all the help it can get, most family farms need the help and effort of every heir *today* just to run the existing operation. So who's got the time to learn accounting or finance? Nobody, for sure, but what price are we paying when we fail to get our heirs the training and experience in business management that they so acutely need for the future?

The education *is* available (see Appendix), but it requires the will to sacrifice something of the present operation for the sake of tomorrow. Management experience is available, too, but that requires taking the risk of giving farm heirs *real jobs*, with increasing responsibility for the management of assets. These are tough choices, but survival and profitability of the family farm require that they be made.

Besides, what better way is there for Dad to pass a few of his three a.m. "blink" sessions to the kids?

HOW DO I GIVE IT ALL AWAY?

Finally, among all his other problems, Dad has to face the issue of what to do with the significant operation he's built.

This is a tough one for him. It's uncomfortable for him to talk about (Mom might think it's his heart again), and nobody else feels it's their place to bring it up (it makes 'em look greedy). But we'll let you in on a secret. Dad does think about it, even though it doesn't seem like he does. And he doesn't much like what he's thinking.

First in his thoughts is the memory that he had to buy it from Granddad. That was a real burden, coming all of a sudden like it probably did, and he's been a little scared ever since.

He walked out on a limb, worked his fingers to their white knuckles, and survived. Now people tell him he's supposed to give it all up!

He talks to financial advisors here and there, and they suggest all sorts of plans for passing the operation on to the kids in some way or other that saves taxes. He hears them. He even nods in agreement. But down the core of his spine, his cells kind of close up with indignation.

*Give it away? I had to buy it. I built it to
what it is today. What about me . . . and Mom?
And I don't know that it's good for the kids to just
get it handed to them without some sweat.*

It's not that he doesn't love his children. Maybe he loves them too much, in fact. He wants the best for them. He doesn't want them spoiled.

God, he thinks, what a problem. And who do I give it to? That's another thing. How can I be fair to my sons who are working the farm and the three kids who aren't? And the youngest might want to work with us when he gets out of college. I don't know if we have enough room for him, especially if John gets married and needs a house.

Much as he might think so, Dad's not alone in these concerns. Every successful farmer smacks up against them sooner or later. In fact, estate planning is such a significant problem, and so universal in family farms, that most of the following chapters will be devoted to it.

But . . . we're not through with the problems. These are just the most striking views Dad sees as he surveys his successful operation. Seeing them, he often thinks wistfully back to Granddad, and wishes wistfully for those vanished, simpler years.

But he thinks, too, of his blessings. They *are* considerable.

Primary among those blessings (believe it or not, Dad) are the farm heirs' spouses. They are a major part of the future of the family farm, and need to be understood and employed effectively like any valuable asset. So, before we start looking at solutions to passing down the farm, we should spend some time understanding the kids-in-law.

---

[1]Harold T. Rogers, "The Business of Farming," *American Vegetable Grower*, August 1985, p. 54.

[2]Randy R. Fiddelke, *"The State of U.S. Agriculture Today,"* Speech before the National Farm Smart Users' Conference, Fall, 1984.

Chapter 6
THE HEIRS AND IN-LAWS

What is it about farmers' sons?

Are they born with an attraction to greedy, aggressive females?

And what about farmers' daughters? Do they have to marry lazy incompetents?

Of course not. Yet, if you listen to Dad tell it, The Kids sure seem to have an appalling lack of matrimonial taste. Well, in some cases this may be true. Usually, however, when Dad complains about his kids-in-law, he's really complaining about the tough time he has getting along with them.

You can be sure the complaint, where it exists, is mutual. If you dare to ask who's at fault in the whole mess, each "aggrieved" party is sure to point promptly to the other. Dad and his kids-in-law can seldom agree on who's done what to whom — nor can they agree about the actual seriousness of the conflict.

For the son- and daughter-in-law, the situation tends to go from difficult to unbearable — mostly because Dad doesn't take things seriously (as far as they can see). "He (Dad) doesn't even see the problem," the kids-in-law say.

They seem to be somewhat right. For Dad, things are

likely to go from nuisance to damn nuisance — and not much farther. His in-law problems never quite become acute. Instead, they settle into a state of chronic annoyance, which he endures in the stoic belief that discomfort with in-laws is a natural part of family life (the way aching joints are an inevitable curse of old age).

This is unfortunate, from both a human and a business point of view. Ignoring festering disagreements between in-laws can generally make life difficult and uncomfortable, but when you add a family business to the formula, the "so what" approach to sons- and/or daughters-in-law has been known to lead to the breakup of a farm operation and the family that owned it.

This might sound like an exaggeration, but it isn't. Few farm owners (and even fewer sons- or daughters-in-law) recognize the influence inherent in the position of the successor's spouse. The fact is, other than Dad, the person with the most power to determine the kind of future a family farm is going to have is *the successor's spouse*.

There are few positions more inherently powerful than sleeping with the prince (or princess). It's a combination kitchen cabinet and bedroom boardroom with a very exclusive membership. When the last words about or against the king are said at night, those words have hours of silent darkness to work into the successor's rather unstable psyche. Dad's got no voice, no vote, and no veto. He doesn't even share the platform. Over a period of years, those last words can build up into a thickening tangle of emotional weeds.

Dad might believe he can ignore his in-laws, but he believes wrong. We would all do well, in fact, to look a little deeper into the problem — especially if we're interested in preserving the future of our family farms. Probably the best way is to run through a "rogues' gallery" of kids-in-law:

FOUR BASIC MODELS OF "SON-IN-LAW"

Dad's son-in-law usually comes in one of four basic models. If the farm owner wants to maintain a productive, harmonious relationship with his daughters' chosen mates, he'd do well to understand the viewpoints and concerns of the particular models in his family "equipment shed."

Most commonly recognized is *the "hired hand" who's married to Dad's daughter, or the son-in-law laborer on the family farm*. We won't say much about this fellow here, because his problems in actually working for Dad aren't all that different from the problems a son or an outside "acquiror" would face.

One major difference exists, though. That's the common prejudice which holds that the guy who married the farmer's daughter is little more than an economic opportunist, using marriage to further his agricultural career. This prejudice isn't insurmountable for him, but it sure can be difficult. Competence and a high performance level tend to help him out of the hole, but even with talent, he faces an uphill battle on his wife's family's farm. Each degree of responsibility is grudgingly given, always salted with suspicion.

The second model, as yet somewhat rare, but growing in numbers, is *the son-in-law working on the family farm whose spouse, Dad's daughter, is the designated farm successor or "crown princess."* This poor fellow combines all the problems of working for Dad with the further problems of being the successor's spouse. On top of all that, he probably works for *her* now!

This guy suffers from a wider range of problems that tend to be independent of each other. Surviving, for him, requires a very resilient and flexible ego, combined with enough confidence to carve out a real role in the farm operation. All the while, he has to maintain the sensitivity to support a spouse who's also a fellow employee, or maybe even his boss. That's a lot to ask of anybody, and Dad would do well to have a lot of patience with this young man. At least recognizing and acknowledging the complexities here are very important steps for all involved.

Model three, also rare but steadily increasing in numbers, is *the husband of a daughter-successor who isn't, himself, involved in the family farm.*

The unique issue with this fellow is related to his career.

When and as his career needs conflict with his wife's, he winds up in conflict with her family. It's often expected (by Dad, of course) that his career will assume second place to his wife's, and too many farm owners choose to ignore the fact that this is a priority with which his son-in-law may not agree. One thing is sure. Whatever priority is set will have to be understood by and agreeable to everybody involved — and *this requires discussion*.

The fourth, and most common, son-in-law model is *the son-in-law who has his own career*, be it grand or not so grand, and who is married to a boss's daughter who, herself, wants nothing to do with a career in the family business.

This young man, assuming his father-in-law follows the most common (if generally misguided) approach to estate planning, is married to a potential minority shareholder. Our culture places him in the role of "champion" of the rights of his spouse, so he's very interested, by marriage, in the progress of the farm operation. Dad may not think he has much reason to care, but he does — *and he will*.

If his career is in business or one of the professions, he's bound to be even more interested — by personal inclination — in the actions of the family farm. As a professional, he tends to be an activist, too. He's more or less used to being assertive. He understands the ebb and flow of funds and the fundamentally neutral ethics of the business world. He's not likely to be satisfied with platitudes, and he sure isn't obligated to share the family's love of the land.

Whatever model a given son-in-law represents, he's an important person in the family structure, someone who is deeply concerned about decisions being made for the future of the farm. Contented, he can be a loyal friend. Unhappy, he may be a formidable opponent indeed.

THE REAL PROBLEM WITH DAUGHTERS-IN-LAW

As important as Dad's sons-in-law are, the most important (and difficult to understand) spouses of farm owner's heirs are the wives of successor-sons. These are the Daughters-in-law of Dad.

(True, the number of daughter-successors is increasing steadily. In fact, it's almost an explosion — and a welcome one. This means, of course, that the ranks of successors' HUSBANDS are swelling as well. Nevertheless, the statistics remain heavily skewed toward male successors, and they'll stay that way for some years to come. The following discussion, therefore, will be about the wives of these successors. However, problems relating to the successor's spouse are not particularly gender specific, and it's worth noting that most of the "hers" appearing below could just as well be seen as "hims.")

Once Dad's daughter-in-law has entered the farm-owning family, it seems to take her almost no time at all to develop a frustrating relationship with her parents-in-law. Somehow, despite her initially pleasant personality and good intentions, she seems almost inevitably to be cast as an obstacle to family peace and harmony.

Most everybody is surprised by this turn of events, and so is she.

Her new role doesn't do much to enhance her image. Here's how we usually hear it: "Our sons, from the time they were this high, got along like you wouldn't believe. They played together, they were close. You couldn't tear them apart. When they got older it was the same. They worked together like a real team . . . *until they married those # !@ %* women!*"

Sure, Dad loves 'em, but they drive him nuts, too. It was much simpler before. Now, his older son is married to a city girl and the younger boy is married to a farm girl. It seems all Dad does is watch the two of them jockey for position. The older girl is uncomfortable on the farm, so she covers that by being assertive. The younger girl worries that her brother-in-law will get the farm just because he went to college and her husband didn't.

Dad asks again and again: Who needs these troubles?

Some of this is explained by her history; even more is explained by her experience with the new family. From her point of view, she *tried* to be nice, but almost from the beginning she was put into a corner, some dusty niche well outside the normal family traffic patterns. Her in-laws seemed to ignore her — when she wasn't being patted on the head, that is.

Oh, Dad will say he tried to get to know her in the beginning, but she "wanted no part of it." She was stubborn. She was opinionated. She was even disrespectful at times. She just didn't fit in, but that was her fault because she trusted nobody.

"If she doesn't trust me," Dad is likely to ask, "why should I bother with her?"

Even when he admits it's in his interest to try to open lines of communication with her, he's so hurt and distrustful himself that the "dialogue" he starts usually takes the form of a unilateral scolding and an attempt to "explain" reality to her. She, in turn, takes this (quite rightly) as a stiff pat on the head, and the pressure in the family cooker builds.

"What else can I do?" Dad grumbles, deciding to avoid the whole problem and leave her alone. She's her husband's problem. Let him tell her how it is. Thus does the "problem" filter downward in the family hierarchy.

And how well does the successor do as her educator? Terribly. In the first place, the situation is already explosive by the time the farm owner's son gets the teaching job. But that's not all. The heir has his own problems and disagreements with Dad, and who else does he have to talk to about those problems other than his wife (and Mom, the "referee")? He's expected to pacify and placate the very person from whom he needs sympathy for *his* problems with Dad.

He can't mediate because he's in the middle of the battle. Dad's not listening to his ideas. Nor is Dad giving him any responsibility or letting him take any risks. How's he supposed to convincingly explain and defend a family farm operation that's causing him so much grief?

Actually, he *does* talk about it a lot — at first: "Dad said 'No!' again." "He just doesn't respect my ideas." "We're always fighting." "He resists everything I want to do, overrules the decisions I make without him, and gets annoyed when I ask for his ideas."

Well, who else can the successor tell about all this? He knows at least his wife will understand.

And she *does* understand — all too well. Problem is, she gets only half of the story, the bottom half.

Her spouse, the successor, feels his love for his father and his family. He knows the love is a constant through all of the problems and frustrations, and it's the fertilizer of his hope and belief in the future. Sure, he's frustrated, but deep down he knows it'll all work out. Is this what he explains to his wife?

Nope. He doesn't get around to it, or can't, or just assumes she'd think it's silly.

Well, she's tough. She's resilient, to be sure. She hopes for the best. She's patient and supportive. But she's also human. Eventually, after months, perhaps years of this, instead of the understanding the successor expects and certainly needs from his spouse, he gets exasperation and growing impatience. More and more frequently, she criticizes him for not standing up for his rights.

Even if he wants to play the peacemaker and forego his "sounding board," he can't. It's usually too late for that. She's been his confidant for years already. She knows what he thinks about Dad. She's heard it all, and now he wants to come and defend the old guy. Try again.

Almost without his realizing it, things stop being simple — long before her frustration shows. By the time he wakes up, farming has become confused with personalities, love is mixed up with demands, and cooperation seems inseparable from sacrifice. Suddenly, he finds that their goals conflict and their values clash, generating an intense heat that seems to split everything into "us" and "them." Oh, they talk about the crops and the rain and all that, but as more time passes for the successor and his wife, the subject of the *future* of the family farm becomes the perennial winner of their Touchy Subject of the Week Award.

Instead of planning their future together, the successor and his wife always seem to end up talking about "Old What's-his-name" and what should be done to convince him to do what he's "supposed to." The successor has anxieties. She has fears. He advises patience. She wants results. All this turmoil keeps them pretty busy — going around in circles, getting nothing done.

As time passes, conversations escalate. The hurt daughter-in-law asks more and more difficult things from her husband who feels he's stuck in a position between her and Dad. He answers her righteous argument with a patient (and fatal) "But, on the other hand, look at it from his point of view . . ." and the nuclear war begins.

The would-be successor, trying to fit a little bit into both camps while mediating between them, dodges ineffectually in the crossfire. Soon, he begins to forget who the good guys are.

His conclusion from all this? Same as Dad's. It's useless to explain. Better not bring up the succession and the farm at home anymore.

Which, predictably, makes matters worse.

HER PROBLEMS — AND SOME SHE CAUSES

In a family farm, the life of the successor's spouse can be confusing, frustrating, and, in some senses, frightening. Her destiny seems to be in the hands of a stone-walling father-in-law, against whom her White Knight seems unable to stand. Most outsiders don't understand this, thinking she has it made — a view shared by her in-laws, who also see her as having a lot more than she had before.

Her in-town critics see her spouse as the heir-apparent to economic royalty. There's this big house and huge yard. No matter that this isn't wealth, just a natural part of operating a farm. Her friends assume her resources are endless (and, of course, "unearned"), so why can't she take a shopping trip to New York or have everybody out for a big fling in her huge yard? Her farm friends, who know more about farm income, still assume she's got it made. After all, she's going to end up with a farm three times bigger than theirs. She watches friends of many years become more aloof and distant with their growing assumptions of her increasing wealth.

As if this didn't make her lonely enough, she and her husband inhabit different worlds. His is the high pressure life of modern agriculture. He faces challenges every day, at times experiencing the excitement of success, and at other times the depression of failure. At night, he comes home exhausted.

If she has a career of her own — and more and more daughters-in-law do — her successes, her failures, even her exhaustion don't seem as consequential as his. Not to his family, anyway. Her job (rarely is it a "career" as far as her in-laws are concerned) just adds another dimension to the problem. The in-laws seem to demand that she be superhuman in supporting her spouse. As she sees herself in their mirror, she's never unselfish enough to allow her spouse unlimited time and energy for his work. After all, he's working on **THE FARM**. She's expected to do all the things that her mother-in-law has always done, even though her mother-in-law probably never worked off the farm.

But even if she doesn't have a career outside of the home, and she focuses her attention and energies on the critical and important jobs of homemaker and mother (one of the few genuinely gender-specific problems of a successor's spouse), her better "fit" into the family hierarchy does little to ease her frustration. She feels she's chosen a partnership with her husband, adding a domestic stroke to the economic oar he has in the water. She wants, needs, and deserves to know what's happening on the farm. It represents her future and the future of her family. That's no small thing.

She wants to find out how his day was and why the operation is draining him of all his energy and spirit. But he often doesn't want to talk about it, remember, which leaves her in the dark. Her needs aren't filled, while what's expected of her never seems to diminish.

She's expected to be understanding, supportive, tolerant of his never-ending days, and forgiving of his oversights. If she has a complaint, she's expected to swallow it to keep peace in the family. If she doesn't understand the operation, she's expected to love it anyway. If she has worries or problems, she's expected to keep them to herself so he won't be burdened.

If she hesitates or objects to any of these expectations — which, because she's human, she almost inevitably does — she's considered "uncooperative," "obstructionist," "obnoxious," "aggressive," and "greedy."

She begins to believe that her husband's whole family is all too ready to see her as a problem, maybe even as one of her husband's "unfortunate" mistakes.

Instead of being integrated into her new family, she becomes "that woman."

The silent, supportive role expected of the daughter-in-law is a carryover from a culture that really no longer exists. No matter how much Dad or Mom might wish it otherwise, young women of today want no part of that kind of feudal society. Today, women tend to see their personal lives in terms of mutual agreement. They consider themselves individuals with the same kinds of needs and rights as their spouses.

They want to be acknowledged as persons in their own right and given the same respect given to anyone else.

WHY DAD CAN'T UNDERSTAND

Few problems on the family farm are single-faceted, however. Dad's got a few shots of his own to fire.

The farm owner would say that women have always been involved in farming. He's smart enough to know that's inevitable and necessary. What he does object to, however, is their opinion that marrying an heir somehow *gives them a say* in how the family farm should be *managed*. He also believes he's being unfairly blamed for problems the heirs might be having, and resents being resented for what he considers to be kind and generous actions. He feels he's been misunderstood.

Dad knows life is tough. He knows he's done nothing but work his tail off for a quarter century or so, building a farm operation that suddenly now has become the symbol of his "tightfistedness." This gets him upset, because, in his eyes, he's given up a lot in his life so that the women around him can have a good and comfortable life.

What hard work should bring, he believes, is some peace and quiet, and support from the people who are reaping the benefits of what he's built. Instead, what he gets is criticism and accusations that he's not being generous enough, or trusting enough, or that he's too secretive about his plans. And to top it all off, he's accused of not taking his daughter-in-law seriously.

Well, let him tell her a thing or two:

"You don't understand — probably never could — what this farm means to us. You don't have any commitment to it and want everything now, things that my wife and I took years to build. Instead of supporting your husband, you seem to spend all of your energy causing trouble."

Dad resents this. He believes everything he's done and everything he's doing is building the future for his spouse, his children, and his grandchildren. Without him, he's convinced, that future just wouldn't exist. So how can his daughter-in-law believe that he's standing in the way of his son? Why can't she understand that the heir needs to learn, and that takes time? Dad can't be replaced overnight.

And as to her complaints about his communicating too little with his successor, of there not being any time for home or family, his response, from the heart, is that this is the way it is. Period. If it weren't for that "demanding" farm operation, there wouldn't even be a home to go home to. If farming were "easy," everyone would be doing it.

Dad resents his daughter-in-law's resentment that he has control over the farm. *It's his!* Worse yet, she not only wants a say in decisions, she thinks she has a *right* to that say. She might try to explain that he's got that wrong, that she thinks her *husband* has that right, but Dad won't accept that.

Dad, with his sense of greater experience and rectitude, tends to be an autocrat. He takes a parental role with his heirs and their spouses, and expects (almost dictates) certain behaviors and beliefs. The heir has years of experience living with

Dad's peculiarities, but his spouse does not. She has no inclination, in other words, to say "yessir" whenever that's required, because she doesn't *know* that Dad's heart is in the right place.

As one farm owner said to us:

> *"You don't know how upsetting it is to spend all the time and energy I spend on this farm, only to have one of these young women call me selfish or egotistical. They take the gift I've given them — a solid business — without so much as a 'thank you.'"*

Since Dad and his daughter-in-law share neither genes nor childhood nor common experience, they clash.

After a few unsuccessful early attempts to "educate" this woman his son married, Dad decides he should maybe ignore her. She'll understand eventually, he figures, and will adapt to the program like everybody else.

Unfortunately, this is about the last thing she'll do — mainly because she expects *him* to do the adapting and understanding.

The inevitable result of all this waiting for the other guy to change is a problem that gets worse while everyone waits, heels in ground, for some magical change of heart. Nobody even attempts preventive maintenance (their righteous protestations to the contrary). In time, the situation becomes almost impossible.

HOW THE KID GETS STUCK IN THE MIDDLE

Most any objective outsider, meeting and talking with a frustrated daughter-in-law, sees something different from Dad's "greedy, pushy female." What the outsider usually sees is an insecure, uncertain young woman who doesn't understand the new life she's gotten into with her husband. All she seems to get are promises and assurances from Dad (when he talks to her at all) that everything is being done for the best. What she gets from her husband, on the other hand, only adds to her confusion.

In the early days of their marriage, she heard his frustrations and complaints. She countered his feelings of inadequacy. His conversation was limited mostly to disgruntled monologues about Dad — what he wouldn't do, teach, let go of, spend, or understand.

Later, as the successor sees the widening rift between his wife and his family — Dad, Mom, his brothers and sisters — he resorts to evasive silences or attempts careful handling and peacemaking. Too late he tries to undo the damage largely brought on by the pain of his early days on the farm. Unwittingly, through his complaints, he's encouraged her to become an unstoppable champion — and through his "diplomacy," he's deprived her of an objective view of the whole truth.

What the successor finds is a spouse who seems to turn more and more against Dad over time. If he thought he was in a difficult position before, his wife's new anger can make it almost impossible. He wants to stay with the farm, but finds himself carried along by a powerful emotional current to the point where he may have to choose between his wife and the family operation.

He's in the middle. His wife has legitimate concerns for her family's security, his career, and their future together. Opposing those concerns squarely (or seemingly so) are Dad's worries about the future of the farm and how it impacts his own future.

The successor is the key to each of their futures, but the "solution" he represents is very, very different for each. It might seem obvious that the basic answer for everybody is the success of the farm, but it's not that easy. Nobody agrees on the definition of success.

Eventually, almost inevitably and after a long time smoldering under the wallpaper, the conflict breaks into the open. With the opening of hostilities, a most important line of communication in the family — and the farm — parts like an undersea cable in an earthquake.

Two major powers are at odds with each other, with no channel available to deal with and lessen the tensions. The successor might attempt to repair the break, but he's got enough problems of his own just staying alive within the operation. He's a referee without uniform, authority, confidence, or rule book — and his whistle just irritates everybody.

We could ask "who's right?" What we'd find in this, as in most conflicts, is that everyone thinks "I am."

There is no "right," in fact. There are only points of view and, with luck (and a little bit of prayer) a shared objective: continuity of a successful farm, managed by a family that is able to get along.

But this takes understanding — and acceptance.

Take the issue of work, for example. A fundamental value that's widely accepted in the business world — particularly in the world of farm ownership — is the value of hard work. It's common for farm owners, especially, to believe the only way to be successful is to work harder and longer than anyone else.

This basic value is generally built into the fabric of every farm-owning family. It's reinforced by the experiences most farm owners undergo while building their operations. They're familiar with long hours, large risks, uncertainties, anxieties, and crises. That, to them, is a price that's paid for success.

But, suspending for the moment any judgment whether this attitude is proper and justified, it's worth asking whether this culture is readily shared by the successor's wife, Dad's daughter-in-law.

It can be, of course, particularly if she grew up in the same kind of environment. But even if she comes from a farm-owning family, there's no guarantee that she assimilated the culture in which she grew up. Many young men and women today believe in the value of hard work, and they don't really believe lunch comes free, but they also see the negative side of hard work and success. What they see — and want desperately to avoid becoming — are successful people who are leading relatively empty lives.

The successor's wife is likely to appreciate the need for commitment to the farm, but she's also likely to defend with great determination, the depth and quality of her personal life. She wants — and will eventually demand — the freedom to define along with her husband what's best for them and their family.

This can cause Dad some severe problems. He knows that she doesn't understand, that she's young, naive, and surely unrealistic. He feels she has little concept of what a gift the farm represents. He tries to make her understand. She doesn't want to be *made* to understand. And so they clash.

This isn't a matter of right or wrong. It's not a matter of facts or evidence. It's a matter of opinion, culture, and personal values. There should be room on every family farm for many different people, value systems, and lifestyles. There should be — but too often there isn't, because most of us find it hard to make room in our own hearts.

GETTIN' ALONG BY GETTIN' ALONG

Once we understand the different worlds people inhabit, it's easier to understand why it's so difficult for people to agree with each other. We could even say that the variations among people are so vast that *agreement* is probably impossible.

Given that, it's better to work toward acceptance, in the hope that understanding might eventually follow. But if it doesn't, the mere fact that we've been able to accept the other people in the family as well-meaning human beings following their own personal compasses makes it much easier to talk to them. Such acceptance can serve very well to repair that parted communication cable.

The trouble is, of course, that most of us have a tough time accepting the possibility that a situation might be viewed in other ways — other than our own, that is. We recognize people are different. That's easy. What's tough is accepting those differences, and accepting the opinions that come from them.

Farm owners have no corner on the intolerance market. They just have the power to be more blunt. But there's nothing to be gained in placing blame for the disagreements between

Dad and his younger in-laws. What's needed is cease fire and solution — and everybody has a part in that.

Dad and Mom should give serious thought to the potential price for insisting that everyone share their point of view. It's worth remembering that their kids-in-law are much more than chance interlopers. They are powers to be reckoned with, real powers, because the future of the farm depends on them, and, of course, they have a significant role in the development of the grandchildren, the next-to-next generation of farm managers.

Can they accept their kids-in-law — and their attitudes — as a given?

On Dad's part, there's a need for recognizing that his daughter-in-law's motivations stem primarily from love and concern for her family (which, by the way, includes *his* son and *his* grandchildren). She wants economic security, sure. Who doesn't? But mostly she hopes that her spouse can use his talents and abilities to be fulfilled in his work. She hopes, too, that he doesn't have to walk forever in the shadow or under the thumb of his father. She knows this is good for nobody, and Dad, in his wisdom, should know it, too.

For her part, the daughter-in-law had better realize that this farm is, in fact, Dad's. Sure, he says he wants to share it, but the timetable is his to set. Sure her husband has ability, but there's a lot to learn. Of course, he must have responsibility if he's going to learn, but the cost of his mistakes will largely be borne by his father. Just as daughters-in-law aren't born greedy and aggressive, farm owners aren't born stubborn and patronizing.

The daughter-in-law is going to have to give thought to the reality of her position. She did, in fact, marry into a family business (not because she saw the benefits, or even the potential problems — she simply fell in love). Farm ownership carries with it all sorts of demands and sacrifices, but there are also many benefits which she tends, too often, to overlook — benefits like a growing investment, career opportunity for her children, a chance at independence for her spouse.

There's a lot to be gained by taking an objective look at the whole picture and making an honest evaluation of how the benefits and sacrifices balance each other. She has to realize, too, that other members of the family have different values and goals. Their priorities aren't necessarily hers. Can she accept that?

The son-in-law needs to think about all this, too, and also his position as guardian of Dad's daughter. Dad's not suddenly going to stop caring about his "little girl," and his standards for her husband's behavior aren't about to change. They're rooted too deeply in love. These are facts.

If the son-in-law doesn't work on the farm, he'll have to learn to understand the gifts coming from his father-in-law and try to accept them as gracefully as possible. If he does work on the farm, he's going to have to understand that his relationship to Dad is generally a combination of acquiror *and* son. He has the burdens of a family relationship without many of the "guarantees" of the blood tie.

The daughter-in-law's husband, the son and heir, needs some education and wisdom, too. Too often he makes the error of deciding the best course is to ease her mind by keeping her uninformed (how can she worry about what she doesn't know?). It seldom, if ever, occurs to him that this will only make her worry more — about the terrible unknown. She's a partner and rates her share of understanding and responsibility.

It's generally a mistake for a successor to attempt to play mediator between his Dad and his wife. The successor doesn't usually see himself in this role, but that's often the effect his behavior has. He practices amateur "diplomacy" (dishonesty by omission) with his Dad and his wife, succumbing to the powerful temptation to try to pour pacifying oil on his family waters in hopes that he can smooth over disagreements.

But it's a costly sin. His influence is precious and limited. If he uses it wrongly, no matter how much "oil" he uses, it won't calm the storm. The rough water will only return.

His job, as a successor, is not to get his father and his spouse to agree with each other. That's up to chance, circumstance, and *them*. While his best interest lies in their accurate understanding of each other's concerns, the real solution to everybody's problems is going to be his success at qualifying as a successor.

His energy should be concentrated on developing his ability to run a growing, profitable farm operation, while he gives his wife's concerns the respect and consideration they deserve.

As in Einstein's revised Universe, on the family farm there is no privileged observer. Observations are relative to the beholder, and realizing this can serve very well to repair that severed communication line between Dad and his "second in command" — not to mention opening some of the closed channels between others in the family.

Chapter 7
WHY DON'T FARM OWNERS RETIRE?

It's very tempting to wonder why it's so tough for a farm owner to retire.

> *"But it isn't,"* Dad will say. *"I want to re-tire. Heck, I've worked real hard all these years and now it's time for the younger folks to take over."*

Sure. And he even has plans — or so he calls them.

In fact, a lot of farm owners have "plans" for their re-tirement — well, they call them plans, but they're little more than fantasies, self-delusions and daydreams. The typical thought is to get in some fishing, or maybe some travel. Farmers "plan," in their various ways, to do in retirement all the things they never could find time for while they were operating the farm.

But if they always wanted to do these things, just why is it that they never found time for them while they were working? After all, if fishing or travel are going to be interesting enough to fill the next 20 years of retirement, why weren't a few hours found for them in the previous 30 or 40?

It's hard to avoid a nagging suspicion. Could it be Dad didn't find the time because he really *didn't want to take the time?*

Could it be, in fact, that most successful farmers simply don't want to quit working?

Yes, it could. Most farm owners, when pushed for an answer, will frankly admit they never want to retire. Those who are less open about it don't want to either, we believe. They just find it difficult to admit, for a number of reasons.

Farm owners, in general, secretly plan to stay on the job until the guardian angel collects their Green Stamps. And they know it — maybe they won't *admit* it, but they know.

Oh, the farm owner talks about all the great things he and Mom will do someday. You know, the Bass Boat or the camper over the Continental Divide. Sometimes it's even a house in Phoenix or a condo in Ft. Myers. Travel, too. Don't forget travel:

> *"When I retire, me and Mom are going to go around the world, to all the places we've never been."*

And never really wanted to see?

This fantasy isn't the sole property of the successful farmer. Most of us play at retirement eventually. We dream about it in occasional idle moments. We pine for it when we're frustrated. But seldom, if ever, do we seriously think about what it means or make actual plans for it.

It's important, though, because it's not only Dad's farm. There are other people involved. Retirement can sometimes weigh heavily on the whole crew, a long-awaited wind shift that never seems to come. Dad's "retirement" can sometimes hang over everything like an emotional smog.

The real difficulty is that everybody else plans their lives around the belief that he will, in fact, do it.

(Everybody else except Mom, that is. She built her life around his almost total preoccupation with the farm, so, for her, his retirement isn't so much an expected event, as a feared possibility. When he retires, she'll be expected to do the same — and totally reorganize a life she already enjoys. But more about this later.)

TYPICAL RETIREMENT "PLANS," AND WHY THEY FAIL

If we watched Dad's *behavior* rather than his hints about his glorious sunset, we'd see that The Boss really doesn't seem to take retirement very seriously at all.

And there's other negative evidence besides his behavior — the typical retirement "plan" of a typical farm owner, for example.

Has anybody survived 20 years of non-stop fishing? At 20 casts per hour, 5 or 6 hours a day, seven days a week, that's just less than 875,000 casts into the lily pads over 20 years. We should hope he has a good arm.

How much can a person stand before he just goes out and kicks a hole in the boat?

Let's get down to the bare wood. Fact is, for most people, in most walks of life, retirement (in the usual sense) is not a good thing, and the successful farmer knows it.

Being intelligent folks, most farm owners simply avoid retirement desperately. Those who don't avoid it either deteriorate in retirement, or they return, inevitably, to the family farm like the buzzards to Hinckley, the swallows to Capistrano, and politicians to Washington after Labor Day.

Why? Because the farm owner's thoughts about retirement are generally unrealistic, impractical, illogical, and unworkable. And for successors, spouses, employees, suppliers, or advisors to act upon those plans, or to plan the future of a family farm around them is about as sensible as planning a picnic in Buffalo in February on the basis of a weatherman's prediction of 80-degree temperatures.

Sure, Dad should know what he wants — but the physical evidence says otherwise. The "picnic" just ain't gonna happen.

QUITTING . . . OR RESTARTING?

It's difficult, in many ways, for somewhat "younger" folk to understand all this. Why is it so tough, they wonder? Dad seems really drawn to the idea and says he's earned it (who can disagree?). From the kids' point of view, even, it looks real attractive to be able to rest on the laurels of a productive and fruitful life.

That's what we're all after, isn't it — success, respect, and an accomplished dream? Most outside observers would be convinced that the family farmer's accomplishments would give anybody pride and satisfaction. How wonderful it must be to sit back and enjoy those victories.

But is it so wonderful? Does Dad, in fact, get his greatest reward from a final pat on the back? Can he really retire in peace and joy knowing he's done everything important he's ever going to do?

Not usually. Dreams aren't supposed to be reached. They're meant to be *passed*. In each functioning person's heart is an ever-present drive to do new things.

Just consider what it really means to have "had" a good life. Generally, it means that:

- *We've more past than future.*

- *Most of the good things are memories, not expectations.*

- *Our admiring "public" is admiring us on the basis of what we've done more than on the basis of what we can, or will do.*

In some senses, having had a good life can be little more cheering than having a well-written epitaph. Both imply that the best part is over.

In reality, the successful farmer is *having* a good life *now*.

These are the good times, with Dad finally in a situation where he is making a reasonable amount of money and can get away some in the winter. He's even more successful than he ever dreamed. But there's a cloud on his horizon. All of his money is tied up in the farm, and that's a *big* reason to stay involved. "Semi-retired," maybe, but involved just the same.

Sure the past was good, but that's the past. Today is what counts, and today is just fine the way it is. He's not resting on any laurels. He's sampling the fruits of his success, maybe, or taking a few moments out for a little harvesting. But resting? Nope. He's still moving just as fast and hard as ever.

He identifies with the farm operation he built. It's identified with him. To break that closeness would be to cut the taproot of his personality. This is why retirement isn't a high point. It's the end of something that's always been one of the most important things in his life.

Some reward.

Retirement, of course, doesn't have to mean being cut off from meaningful work. It could, instead, be a move to something new, something with the same kind of potential the farm had decades before, when Dad began his career. In a vague sense, this is what Dad wants and needs in retirement. But does he look for it? Does travel have that kind of potential? Fishing? Cribbage?

Possibly for a rare few — but we've yet to meet one.

STAYING IN THE COMBINE IS NO ANSWER

Maybe it's okay that his retirement plans aren't all that firm, Dad might say. So I don't retire. It's my farm. What's wrong with staying active and involved throughout life?

Nothing. But we're not talking about a hobby. We're talking about Dad's continuing, active involvement on the *family farm*. That's a whole different set of issues.

First of all, there's the problem of being smothered by experience. A growing farm operation requires new ideas. It should attract managers who want to invest energy in those new ideas, directions and projects, and who have the time to make them happen. Dad has every intention of going along with all this, but as time passes the farm's future farther and farther outruns his own relaxing pace.

For the younger operator, a fresh idea is a new path to be explored. For the older farmer, a fresh idea implies that much of what he's learned over the years will have to be questioned — and very likely changed, diminished, or expanded.

It's usually true that Dad is better than anyone else at what he does best. He got there by developing some highly specific skills — to the general exclusion of others. His skills are his major intellectual possessions, so the truths he holds to be self-evident (and there tend to be many of them), he can't, by definition, question.

After all, he is, by definition, the experienced specialist.

Is it merely a coincidence that the older we get, the more likely we are to complain about the state of things today? We can't really blame it on the times. Older folks have been saying the same things for thousands of years.

No, it's not a coincidence. It just shows that the older we get, the more we value the time when we were growing, when our future was still a future, when we were striving and building toward our goals.

"Those were the days," we say more and more often as the years pass. And the more today is different from yesterday, the more those *were* the days — passed, gone, never to be repeated.

WE EACH NEED A NEW DREAM

As people become successful and learn more about the work they're doing, that knowledge often locks them in. They know too much, they've seen too much, they've done too much to have any new solutions.

When we're younger, we tend to approach problems with a belief that there are clear-cut solutions. Later, as we learn more about those problems, we get humble. Black and white become increasingly gray, with few, if any, clear solutions.

The farm owner is no exception to this. As he gets older, he walks along inside an ever-narrowing canyon. If he doesn't change direction soon enough and with enough foresight, he eventually finds himself closed in by his own experience.

He can't go on because his path becomes too narrow to travel. He can't change direction because the walls of his experience press in on him from both sides. And he can't retrace his steps because there simply isn't enough time or energy to go back and begin again.

The only answers that seem open to him, then, are:

> (1) *"Retire" into a vacuum, or*
> (2) *Hold on and struggle against the rebellious youngsters who want to overthrow the old ways.*

The first option — retirement into a vacuum — isn't really an option. It's more of a temporary daydream that has the same negative result (long-range) as option 2.

If, on the other hand, Dad insists on Option 2, and stays in his job, his overdeveloped skill *in his specialty — operating the farm —* can have some severe consequences for that farm and for his heirs.

His heirs, you see, have a relative advantage over him — at least with respect to the farm operation. They have the time to get involved and can over-spend their energy. They're not weighed down by Dad's "baggage," either. They have less idea what "can't be done." They're only beginning the process of setting their experience into concrete.

Look at it another way. New ways tend to come easier to someone mastering a skill than to the proven master. Sure, the master knows all the complexities of his craft, but that very mastery makes it tough for him to try something new. It's too much like beginning farming all over again.

Oh, he keeps up religiously with all the progressive techniques of farming. He will use any kind of advanced technology necessary to be more productive in the field or in the barn, but he will typically say, "I'll let *them* learn the computer . . ." Dad has no problem learning more about the farm, but the *business* of farming is something that is difficult for him to swallow.

The farm owner is committed by the vastness of his experience to the farm as an agricultural operation. The heir shares that commitment, too, but is also new enough to begin to struggle with the business concepts. The successor is more likely to have the fresh eye needed to recognize what needs changing, as well as new opportunities. And isn't that freshness the very thing that led to Dad's original success?

ALTERNATIVES TO THE TRASH HEAP

All right, neither of Dad's options work. So what's he supposed to do?

It seems like a hopeless dilemma. Most of us don't want to retire, and if we do, we do it without enough planning to avoid disappointment. Yet, if we stay with what we do well, we inevitably become less and less creative in our skill. Can't retire. Can't stay. Now what?

Quite a lot, actually.

The question of retirement isn't really a matter of either/or at all, because there are more than two options (yes or no) available. The real trick is finding ways to uncover those other possibilities.

To begin with, throw the word "retirement" out of your working vocabulary. In its classic meaning, "retirement" implies withdrawing from work, business, public life (and life in general?). It's not an option. It's actually more of an unfortunate fate we should try to avoid.

To stop doing is to die (maybe not physically, although we've all seen sad examples of just such a result), but to keep doing the same thing long past the time the edge is lost can be just as destructive.

The decision not to "retire" doesn't necessarily imply that we have to stay in our present occupation. Change is the soil of growth, so it seems obvious that chronic resistance to change is an almost certain sign of decline. Change is the stuff of fun and excitement — and an extender of time. Remember the endless summer days of childhood? The repeating newness had a way of slowing down the passage of time as we were awed by the life around us.

Change doesn't have to be discouraging, not if it's the kind of change we want. Nor does stability mean real comfort — not if it's only another way to say "stagnation."

There is an answer to the retirement dilemma: AVOID THE PROBLEM. The alternatives aren't limited only to "keep doing" or "stop doing." *The answer is to do something else* — to find ways we can keep alive the excitement and fun that allowed us to work hard enough to become successful.

This is true for all of us, but it's particularly important for the farm owner. The health of his business and the commitment of his heirs depend on his ability to find that acceptable new career. Master craftsmen must make way for the journeymen.

Sound business plans, qualified successors, and agreeing spouses are all important for the future of the family farm, but figuring out where Old Dad is going, and where he wants to go in "retirement" is even more important. It's important for Dad's health, the successors' sanity, and the sustained growth of the operation.

In family farms that have been passed down smoothly, a key factor in that success was finding a way for the present farm owner to become the "former" farm owner. Those who've done it right have managed to get it done sometime before people start saying *"Shame He Waited So Long."*

But — and we can't overemphasize this "but" — just stepping out of the flying airplane so somebody else can have a chance at the controls is no solution. Dad can't really leave unless he has somewhere to go — and no loyal member of his family would want to see him wander off into a desert.

We'll look into where Dad can go in the next chapter.

Chapter 8
WHAT IS REAL RETIREMENT?

In the previous chapter, we managed to confuse Dad, somewhat, and to discourage the heirs by saying that a successful farmer should "never" retire.

Well, we have to confess that we overstated our case a little to make a point. Actually, it's not retirement we're against. It's "Pseudo-Retirement," the kind that's neither real nor sensible. What we're really pushing for is "Real Retirement," which in most cases is a change in occupation rather than the ending of a career.

We've seen many Real Retirements, and most of them worked very well. But it wasn't an accident that they worked. They worked because they were put together right. While it's true that there are as many types of retirement as there are successful farm owners, the good plans all seem to have the same basic features.

ESSENTIAL FEATURES OF REAL RETIREMENT

We call these basic features of successful retirement plans the Components of Real Retirement. There are four of them:

1) **Real Retirement solves the retiree's security problems.**

A primary reason why many farm owners want to keep control of their operations is to make sure somebody else doesn't mess up their investment.

"Sure," Dad says, *"I'll get out of the way and let the kids run it — but I want to know everything they're doing, and I want the ultimate veto. Everything I have is in this farm."*

The concern is justified, of course, and if Dad has no choice but to keep his assets tied up in the farm, the desire to maintain control would be justified, too. But, in more cases than farm owners think, it's not necessary to risk the assets on successor managers. The growth as well as the risk can usually be moved to the shoulders of the young.

This isn't an estate planning book, but we *are* concerned with options here. Probably the best few hundred bucks or so Dad could spend would be to take a good attorney or life underwriter out to lunch and just let him brainstorm about options available for protecting assets while giving the heirs ownership. More than likely, Dad will be so astounded he'll forget to eat his pork chops.

Sure, we're well aware how tough it can be to find good advisors. We don't mean to oversimplify the complexity of getting good advice. In fact, the last chapter is devoted to nothing but this problem. But, meanwhile, the point should be well taken — few plans can be put together successfully without top-notch professional help.

Estate planning techniques can take many forms. Just a few examples of approaches will be listed here as examples:

● **RECAPITALIZATION:** This is a whole family of methods for reorganizing the kinds of stock issued by the company for the purpose of separating ownership of assets from control of the farm. This can be accomplished with an existing corporation or a new corporation or partnership created for the purpose.

Commonly, recaps are done primarily to allow more flexibility in shifting assets from one generation to another. There are many ways to go about this, but the most common approaches usually involve converting common shares into a mixture of voting/non-voting stock, which allows the farm owner to place management control wherever he wants it (yes, he can also keep it in his own hands), while equity can be shifted to the next generation.

The present owner, for example, could keep his voting shares and direct their transfer to the successor(s) in his will after the Persistent Reaper has superseded Dad's need for security. The existence of non-voting shares can allow him much more flexibility in distributing equity and future growth.

This sort of approach, combined with a gifting program, can do a lot to solve the farm owner's fear of losing control, but it can have one disadvantage. Improperly designed, it can keep management control in the present owner's grip, thus keeping him tied to the operation of the farm. While this may fit Dad's plans, it's unlikely to fit the long-term plans of the successors.

Fortunately, there are ways to set up systematic gifting or sale of the voting stock to the heirs on an incentive basis. We won't go into those approaches here, because this whole issue requires the help of a competent professional familiar with the specific situation. Again, good advice is essential.

- **INSTALLMENT SALE:** What if Dad really wants to free himself of concern about the day to day operation of the farm so he can pursue his new career? What if the successors have more taste for risk than he, and want to *grow*? Using this technique, the farm owner can transfer control of the farm to his successors, while at the same time protecting his security.

Typically, the heirs buy the farm on an installment basis. The principal benefit of an installment sale is the creation of a stream of income for the length of the sale — 10 years, 20 years, whatever. This provides Dad with his needed retirement income, using the farm assets as collateral. The farm continues on much the same as far as the neighbors can see, except that Dad has "sold out to the kids."

The successor managers form a new company, to which the old company sells its key operating assets for a long-term note. The real estate and equipment could be made available to the new company through a lease, thus keeping ownership of those assets in the hands of the present owners.

Through this approach, the original company is turned into a holding company owning assets and generating cash. The operating risks are transferred to the new company — actually, the successors — accomplishing the major goals of both the present and future owners.

This technique isn't particularly new. Its been used over and over again by hundreds of thousands of farms over the last 100 years. The major difficulty, however, is that what used to be a very common event doesn't often work well on either a cash flow or a tax basis. The reasons are too complicated to get into here in any detail, but installment sales have taken a bad beating from the changes in land values, the decline in commodity prices, and the wild fluctuations in interest rates.

• **CREATING A SUBSIDIARY:** In cases where the present owner has some major disagreements with the direction the successor managers want to go, he could protect himself, while giving them their heads, through the establishment of a subsidiary company. This is not a particularly common approach with family farms, but the ideas are worth covering anyway.

In the most common situation (as in the Mackey case), the present owners will use the farm to guarantee a loan or loan money outright to a son or daughter for investment. This makes it possible for the heirs, through the use of borrowed money, to increase their own net worth. This is a method for enhancing the wealth of the family as a whole through the use of the assets of the senior generation.

If there are no on-farm heirs in the family, a first step in succession planning could be to create a new entity for the heirs in their chosen field, and fund it partially through a transfer of the farm to non-family successors.

- **DEFERRED COMPENSATION.** This approach simply involves a salary continuation agreement which allows Dad to get an income for some defined period of time, in addition to his other retirement provisions (Keogh, etc.). Deferred compensation plans don't require the transfer of all of the assets of the business, although such a transfer usually occurs eventually and has no effect on the deferred compensation.

Salary continuation plans are simply exchanges of promises. Dad promises to continue to work for the company, not to compete after retirement, and perhaps be available for consultation after retirement. The company, for its part, promises to pay him cash.

There are tax advantages and disadvantages to these plans, as you might guess, not to mention the risk Dad is taking by becoming just another creditor of the farm. But, in general, deferred compensation plans are too seldom used by successful family farms, usually because the required technical advice isn't available, or is poorly used.

The point of these examples is not to *recommend* one or the other of the techniques. The tax and business implications are too complex to be adequately dealt with in this kind of overview. But they should demonstrate, in a small way, the varied options available to achieve ownership transition with controlled and defined risk.

Security needs can be handled with planning and competent professional help. One thing is sure: if they're not handled, Dad's "retirement" plan has about as much viability as a gnat at a toad convention.

2) **Real Retirement absorbs the retiree's creative energies.**

A few years ago, we met a farmer and his three sons who'd worked out a neat solution to the retirement question. This owner manager had founded a successful vegetable operation in the Midwest. After 15 years of building a respected and profitable business, however, he found himself becoming stale. It wasn't the fun it used to be, and he was spending more and more of his time administering the farm — something he disliked (and, predictably, didn't do well).

Fortunately (and this wasn't a matter of luck), his three sons were competent, ready, and wanted their chance at running the operation. But where would Dad go?

He'd had that answer in mind for a couple of years. Wine (fermenting, not drinking) had become a major hobby of his over the previous five years. He'd even imported some specialized vines from a vintner he knew in Ohio and had begun the tricky job of raising them in Michigan's "unique" grape-growing climate.

He believed his knowledge of farming, combined with what he thought was a good feel for the tastes of his neighbors, would result in a successful local winery. As his vines began producing, he began experimenting with the complexities of fermentation.

In a variation on the "growth subsidiary" theme, he gave control of the vegetable operation to his sons in exchange for a cash investment in the new winery he owned and controlled. Both operations are successful today. In fact, the winery's doing so well that Old Dad's beginning to face the same administrative headaches he'd experienced with the original operation. The odds are good there's a new "retirement" venture brewing somewhere on his horizon.

Creativity can be absorbed in many ways. They don't all have to be as ambitious as a new venture. We've seen examples of restaurateurs who passed the business over to the kids and spent their time making specialties at table side, talking with the customers. We've seen business owners who went back into the lab to their first love: developing new products. We've seen new charities founded and funded, or hospitals built and managed. We've seen books written, consulting firms formed, and fallow farmland reclaimed.

The key to every one of these new careers, however, was the fun and challenge they represented to the person "retiring." That's why they worked.

3) **Real Retirement allows the successor-managers to have their heads.**

Just as Dad has to go somewhere, someone has to be around to fill his old job, bringing with them the required commitment, energy, and talent. If Dad leaves in theory but not in practice, the message is sent that nothing has really changed. And, in fact, nothing really has. The buck still stops in Dad's lap and nothing's been done except to make an unfortunate situation worse.

Dad would probably have failed trying to work for someone else. He's an operator, not an employee. His success stemmed from the freedom, flexibility, and responsibility that managing his own farm allowed him.

Successor-managers to a family farm need this same freedom because an independent spirit is a critical part of their successful development. If they're forced too long to work under the owner's watchful (and somewhat skeptical) eye, it's unlikely they'll work any better than the hired hands they are.

A retirement where Dad keeps control over his supposedly qualified successors is no retirement at all.

4) **Real Retirement fits Mom's needs and desires.**

Unfortunately, usually the last person considered in the process of "retirement" planning is the spouse of the retiree. In most family farms, this spouse happens to be a wife, but the problem applies equally to the husband of a retiring woman. The question has to be asked: whose career change is this, anyway?

Too often, wives of farm owners confess to us their concern about Old Dad's plans. *"He's talking about retirement, and I just don't know what I'm going to do with him if he does."*

These women have built their own lives while Dad was busy working the farm. They have careers. They have volunteer activities. They have their friends and their grandchildren. In many cases, they work on the family farm and might want to keep doing so.

But Dad gets it into his head that it's time to move to Florida, or travel around the world, or go fishing (Mom, of course, stays in the cabin and cooks). Needless to say, none of these ideas holds an automatic attraction for Mom. Not only does she suspect they're not right for Dad, she's also positive they're not right for her.

Dad will have to find a new career, and that will have some effect on Mom. Isn't it reasonable that she should have some say in his decision, considering how it will effect them both?

Retirees, like successors, come in couples.

THE 10 COMMANDMENTS OF RETIREMENT

These are the challenges of that bittersweet stage of life called "retirement." It's at once a curse, a necessity, an opportunity, an unlikely event, and the wrong word. It should probably be called something else — shift in direction, renewal, career change — but the term we give to it isn't as important as how we approach it.

Each of us — whether we are farm owners, heirs, successors, or spouses, — should keep before us these "10 Commandments of Retirement:"

I. **THOU SHALT NEVER RETIRE.**

Seems like a contradiction to make the first commandment of retirement an order not to do so, but that's how it is.

II. **THOU SHALT NOT STAY FOREVER IN THY JOB**

This is a sort of converse of Commandment I. The decision not to stop doing doesn't imply continuing what's being done today. Law and accounting firms have an unwritten rule about career potential: "Up or out." For the farm owner, it should read "Up and out, and on and on." Don't quit, but don't stand still either. There is only one direction we can coast.

Dad should, in short, separate his future from the future of the operation he's leaving. If he doesn't do this, his future won't be his to control.

III. **THOU SHALT TEACH THOSE WHO FOLLOW, BUT NEVER, NEVER CONSIDER IT SUFFICIENT.**

In the best of all possible worlds, the older generation passes its wisdom and experience on to the younger generation. This is fine, and a wonderful thing.

It's also next to impossible for parents to do for children.

Any father, for example, who's tried to teach his son or daughter how to drive learned very quickly how difficult it is to *teach* one's own offspring. And if it's tough to teach the simple skill of driving, how much less likely will it be that Dad can teach his heirs how to run the farm?

If and when we find ourselves frustrated by our students, it is a far, far better thing we do to leave their training to someone else. The best teachers know when to back away from the student.

There's nothing the matter with kids today that wasn't natural for kids in any day. The "matter" is in the tired eyes of the teacher who can't get beyond memories of early mistakes to see his student in an ever-widening light.

IV. **THOU SHALT PROVIDE FOR COMPETENT TEACHING OF THY HEIRS.**

A direct consequence of Commandment III (the hint that we might not be the best teachers for our offspring) is the need to find somebody else to do the job. In the case of the family farm, these teachers can be other farm owners, 4H, FFA, the agricultural college, or even an in-town agricultural business.

Generally, it's easy to teach the kids how to farm. There are a lot of sources for that training. But we also have to teach them how to manage — and that training is not so easily found around the family farm. This need underlines the value of outside experience.

(It would be nice, of course, if Dad could find students of his own, because he has much to teach and it's good for him to do so. And he'll be amazed at what good students *other* people's kids can make. By the way, for some reason, grandchildren make *great* students.)

V. **THOU SHALT SEEK THE ADVICE, COUNSEL, AND AGREEMENT OF THY SPOUSE.**

Just as successors come as couples, so do farm owners. None of us operate in a vacuum, nor are we islands of career planning unto ourselves. We do things together, or we're probably not going to do them at all (not for very long, anyway).

This isn't to say that retirement should be a joint career for Dad and Mom. If they don't have a joint career prior to "retirement," there's no particular reason why they should have one after retirement. After all, what they're moving to probably won't be all that different from what they're leaving. Each has a life to lead, only now there may be more time available to do things together.

VI. **THOU SHALT AVOID SEEKING WHAT THOU AVOIDED IN THE PAST.**

We do what we like and prefer, most of us. If there's a dream that's never really been chased — writing that book, developing that hobby, building that ferro-concrete boat for sailing around the world — there's probably a reason why. Don't expect things to change all of a sudden.

It's possible, but the odds are slim.

VII. **THOU SHALT AVOID "SEMI-RETIRE-MENT."**

This is a solution many a farm owner has hit upon as the answer to his retirement dilemma. It's really little more than an underhanded way to hold onto his job until the Eternal Bank calls his loan. It can also have the side effect of fooling the successors and heirs into thinking something positive has happened — until, of course, "He's BACK!"

More likely, the kids will feel like migrant laborers in the summer and caretakers in the winter. Semi-retirement, as they soon learn, is an illusion.

Often, the person most fooled is the retiree.

VIII. **THOU SHALT BE COMFORTABLE WITH THE NEED TO PROTECT THY INVESTMENTS.**

It's tough sometimes to break habits and values that have been operating for decades, but the risk/reward system does not operate the same for the old as it does for the young. It's important to become more comfortable with wanting more rewards as we grow older. Risk is for youth. Young people can recover from losses that would be near-terminal for people in their sixties and seventies.

Some farm owners find it tough to admit or accept that they're not all that confident in letting their heirs or younger managers handle their assets. But being conservative with the future of a hard-built operation is anything but a sign of decline. It's common sense, a result of some new priorities that come with the passage of time.

The reason each of us should plan for Real Retirement is not only to make room for the coming generation. The main reason for Real Retirement is the protection of our financial security by passing *risk* onto others, thereby (we would hope) lengthening the span of a useful and interesting life.

IX. **THOU SHALT DISCUSS THY PLANS WITH THY FAMILY.**

They have more than a passing interest, after all. A time-table can help greatly.

X. **THOU SHALT FOLLOW THY PLAN.**

And this is the hard part.

What's usually called "retirement" is not the end of something. It's a continuation of the growth process that begins at birth. Only the emphasis changes with time.

Early in life, our job is to acquire experience in a world that is entirely unknown. Later, we have to learn to break free of our experiences and find new worlds to explore. Our taste for complexity and diversity declines. Quality becomes more important. Our time horizons narrow, but the view around us improves to magnificence.

Retirement is not something that "happens" to us. It is something we do — and had better do *well* — because coming back to running the farm is never really going to be an answer.

Chapter 9
DIFFERENT PEOPLE — DIFFERENT GOALS

One of the results of success in family farming is usually a steady increase in the number of family members working the farm. The successful farm owner, like most other people, increases, multiplies, and fills his earth.

This is a blessing. Family is a blessing, as is the chance to work with people we know, love, and trust.

But it can also be a curse if it's not managed with understanding and patience.

The major question facing successful family farms is not a question of farm prices, land values, or cash. It's a question of whether or not all these people can keep the thing together.

Once a farm enters the third and following generations, the number of players can grow astoundingly. The operation went from Granddad, to his five kids (only some of whom stayed on the farm), thence to grandchildren and even great grandchildren (even fewer of whom are likely to be on the farm).

Ownership goes from a founder to brothers and sisters, to cousins, to distant relatives. The relationships are less and less close, while the complexity of the problem grows like weeds.

We had a client family in which the operation was owned by two brothers, their sister, and a sister-in-law, who had recently been widowed. One of the brothers wanted to retire. The other already had. Through this struggle, they were working at buying out the interest of the deceased brother — and running out of cash doing so.

That was all complex enough. But this was a family farm, remember. The third generation was already on line — six cousins (and a fourth generation just entering their teens!)

The present owners looked off over the land and wondered how the others were going to buy them out — and what would happen if something bad occurred while they were trying to do it.

This happened to be a large, expanding operation. They had a large farm and a processing plant. There were (so far) enough businesses for all these different people to fit into, but the complexities of their relationships to each other were beginning to get out of hand.

This is not an unusual situation for the family farm by any means. By the nature of rural life, the family farm is probably one generation ahead of all our other businesses. Thus, typically, there are usually a lot of people involved — and the natural question inevitably arises: what do we do with all these people? Everybody in the family is in one way or another attached to that farm.

WHY ARE WE DOING IT?

It would be tough for anyone — anyone who's familiar with the family farm, at least — to deny that passing down a successful farm operation intact is one of the most complicated, frustrating, and difficult tasks human beings can take on.

Even at its best, life on a family farm is not without stress. A successful operation puts a lot of pressure on a family. It amplifies the normal frustrations of family life, while it demands so much more from the people. And the real trouble comes from one major cause — the tendency among farm families to avoid the important questions. They fail to communicate about the most important issues they face.

Still, despite the problems, families attempt farming together by the hundreds of thousands every year. Millions of people are going through the preliminaries (or post-mortems in too many cases) every day. And, even more remarkable, many of these prospective heroes actually *succeed*.

Family farms do perpetuate, generation to generation, and they do so primarily because the people within the owning families have the commitment, the guts, and the energy to stick out the process. But that still leaves us with the central question: *Why* do they stick it out?

We try to explore people's reasons for sticking it out every chance we get — individually, in professional relationships with clients, and during family farming seminars. We've compared experiences with other professionals in the field. After doing this for a long time, one very remarkable fact has emerged — very few members of families in farming hang in there primarily because the farm is a good financial investment.

This isn't to imply family farms are bad investments, but it does indicate financial return is a relatively minor reason for staying in a family farm operation. In fact, the family farm is more typically seen as an illiquid investment with very little mobility.

So why do they stay?

The reasons seem to be as different as human beings are themselves. In some cases, the reasons are conscious. In most cases, though, they're first thought about when the question "Why?" is asked.

Most people seem to simply go through day after uncomfortable day, vaguely feeling that something isn't right. Sometimes they're in great emotional pain. On the other hand, those who are happy and fulfilled by working on their family farms seldom stop to consider why their operations work.

If a journalist were to interview the members of a typical

family owning a farm, he would hear as many different answers to his basic question (*"Why is a nice person like you in a situation like this?"*) as there were people he interviewed:

"WHY" AS MOM AND DAD SEE IT

INTERVIEWER: *You look tired, frustrated, and even driven to distraction, sir. Why do you keep it up? You look like you have enough laid aside for yourselves and the future.*

DAD: That's a good question. I guess I'm doing it for my family, particularly the kids. It's my legacy to them, a gift of my work and sweat over the years. If it wasn't for the kids, I suppose I would've sold out years ago. Granddad did it for me. He wanted me to do it for my kids. Now there are my grandchildren.

It's probably not worth the hassle otherwise.

I: *Things have really been that rough?*

D: Sure. We've gone through a lot of really tough years, years when prices were terribly depressed, weather was bad, and interest rates were high.

Frankly, I'm a little tired of it — very tired, in fact. If I wasn't needed to hold it all together until the kids are ready, I'd be sitting in my Bass Boat up at Clear Lake, retired and taking it easy.

I: *But what about you? Aren't you getting anything out of farming or out of working? Isn't there something about the operation that's keeping you going?*

D: Oh, I still enjoy some parts of it. But that's not the point. The farm is going to be theirs someday, and what they need is me out of their way. I've already let them buy in — a little — and each of them is going to get a quarter of the whole pie after I'm gone. I feel I have to protect that for them.

I: *What about you, Mrs. Farm Owner? Why do you stay involved with the business?*

MOM: Mainly, I stick with it because my husband does. This farm is something he's always loved. He's worked it with his bare hands for 40 years, and I've always supported him. Now, I feel we have to support the kids. It's been our life.

I: *Was the family farm good for your family?*

M: Yes. Farming is good for any family, assuming (chuckle) you've all taken the vow of poverty. But our problem now is not getting along together as well as we used to. There do seem to be a lot more fights than before, especially between our children who work with Dad and their brother and sister who don't. And now that our son-in-law came with us, it's getting even more complicated.

Still, I can see everybody's point of view, and everybody deserves a chance.

I: *Well, maybe all those problems mean your family should really get out of farming and do something else.*

M: No. I want to hold the farm together so that all our children can have the opportunity their father and I built for them, not just the two who are working it. That's what a family is for — and that's why we all have to learn to get along better than we do — and why we have to hold this farm together.

"WHY" AS THE KIDS AND THEIR SPOUSES SEE IT

I: *Your parents tell me they're sticking with the farm so it can be yours someday. Why are you still involved?*

THE WORKING SON: Because I've always wanted to farm, and I know they're doing it for me, I guess. That's not an easy thing — knowing that, I mean. I really appreciate what they've done and don't want to let them down.

Sure it's tough. I've been working for Dad all my life, it seems, and it never gets any easier. Nor do the answers seem any closer. But it would be stupid for me to change now, after all that emotional investment. And, besides, I've learned a lot about farming.

I could never buy my own farm, and if I changed careers now, I'd lose all that experience and time I've invested here, and have to start over.

I: *But what about the early years, when you were still flexible enough to move if you wanted to?*

TWS: Truth is, I never was all that flexible. That's some-

thing my wife never understood. First of all, farming is all that
I've ever done. I didn't have any other experience, except the
Army. And, besides, there are a lot of other things to think about
over and above my career.

I: *Such as?*

TWS: The rest of the family, for one thing. My brother
and sister who aren't working here. Someone has to keep it going
for them. And then there's Mom and Dad. It would kill them if
this farm folded up or were sold to some stranger.

I: *But do these reasons justify the effort you put in?*

TWS: I don't think that's the point right now. Eventually
Dad'll decide to let go, and when that happens — when I'm
running things — there'll be a lot of time to reap the rewards of
my investment. Meanwhile, I'm learning how to become a
farmer in my own right.

I: *What about you, Dad's daughter-in-law. You don't have
the same ties to the farm or the family as your husband does.
Why are you still agreeing to your husband's involvement?*

THE WORKING SON'S SPOUSE: I'm only doing it
because my husband wants to stick with it. As far as I can see,
though, his father doesn't respect his judgment in managing the
farm, never gives him any credit or responsibility, and is never
going to pass along the farm.

I: *What if your husband simply asked you what to do?*

TWSS: If it were up to me (and if we could afford it),
we'd quit tomorrow and do something else. Well, it's not that
simple. I like living and raising the kids here on the farm, but
with all the money and other pressures, I really wonder sometimes. It's not up to me, anyway.

I: *What about you, The Boss's daughter-successor? You're
working with your dad, your brother, and your brother-in-law.
Why?*

THE WORKING DAUGHTER: Because the farm is
important to the family. It always has been. That's mainly why
I'm here. I had a perfectly good career in teaching for five years
before I came in, but I could see that the farm was in trouble.

My husband thinks I'm crazy. He says I could be making more money and enjoying myself more back at the high school, and maybe he's right. But he doesn't understand how important this farm is to my family. I couldn't just stand by and watch it go under.

I: *You're her husband. Is that enough reason for you?*

THE WORKING DAUGHTER'S SPOUSE: It's what my wife wants to do, although, God knows, I don't understand it. I mean, what's a high school teacher doing raising cows?

I'm going along with it because there's a lot of money involved in the land and I figure she's protecting her investment (and maybe her mother's).

And, boy, does it need protecting. I don't have a lot of faith in agriculture. I don't think her brother knows what he's doing, no matter how much Dad wants him to run the place, and I think her father's management ideas are somewhere back in the Stone Age.

I: *But doesn't that make the family farm a shaky investment in your mind?*

TWDS: Sure, but who knows, it might work out — and if it does, you can never tell.

Heck, I might get a job on the farm, too.

"WHY" AS OFF-FARM HEIRS AND THEIR SPOUSES SEE IT

I: *You're an heir and not working for your Dad. But your husband is. That seems like a difficult road. Why do it?*

THE NON-INVOLVED DAUGHTER: I don't know that much about the farm. I'm a pharmacist. But I do feel it's a great opportunity for our children. That's why my husband is working for Dad, kind of to keep an eye on things and make sure our rights are protected. Dad asked him to come in when he was looking for a job, and I guess we feel some gratitude for that, too.

I: *So your husband hasn't had any problems.*

TND: Oh, don't get the wrong idea. My husband's had

some problems with my brother and sister, and Dad seems to assume my brother will eventually be the one to run the farm, but I think in a few years my husband will prove himself equal to those two, even though they've been in longer.

I'm worried about my brother and my husband when Dad isn't here to keep things in hand. What if my husband ends up taking orders from my brother?

I: *But there's a good chance it'll happen the other way around. What happens then?*

TND: Then my brother will have problems, I guess. Still, we'll stick to it because we have as much right to benefit from the farm as my brother and sister. It shouldn't make any difference to my husband's chances that I want to stay home with our children.

I: *Do you agree with your wife?*

THE WORKING SON-IN-LAW: I think so. Maybe I should've stuck to teaching, but I could see that things were getting out of hand on the farm and that our kids stood a chance of being cut out of their inheritance.

As far as I'm concerned, my wife has a right to stay home and raise the kids if she wants to, and that decision is no reason why she shouldn't have a say in what happens. After all, she's an owner, just like her brothers and sister.

I: *But they've been treated differently?*

TWSIL: You bet. They were taking salaries out and we couldn't. It just wasn't fair. That's why I'm working here now.

I: *What about you two?*

THE OFF-FARM SON: My brother was trying just the other day to talk me into selling my share to him when Dad dies. I mean, I thought that was cold-blooded as hell.

Besides, does he think I'm stupid? I can see the operation growing. I can see that land values can only increase, even though slower than they used to. Maybe I'm not getting anything out of it now, but I know that later on that farm is going to represent a significant chunk of change. I'm holding on for that day.

THE OFF-FARM SON'S SPOUSE: Someday that farm is going to be worth a lot of money — assuming my in-laws don't screw it up beforehand.

I agree with my husband, we have a right to our share.

10 TYPICAL "WHYS" — AND WHY THEY FAIL

These fictional people represent a composite family farm, a typical grouping of relatives and relationships all circling a successful operation like moths around a flame. There are many possible combinations, of course, but what the above people said is a pretty good sample of what these people think.

Please notice a few remarkable things in what they said.

Most striking is the almost complete lack of enthusiasm. It's the most telling symptom of important "Whys" left unanswered. These people remain "on" their family farm not so much by choice as out of a feeling that they somehow *should*. For Dad — and his successor, if he's the "right" one — there's also the belief that it will all, somehow, work out.

Just how well do the typical "shoulds" stand up to hard scrutiny, though?

WHY # 1: *"If It Wasn't for the Kids."*

While there's little doubt that human beings regularly and naturally make sacrifices for their kids, sacrifice isn't the only human drive. Farmers stick with their farms for more reasons than legacy-building.

If Dad were just interested in the future of his children, he would do everything possible to plan the farm's future. His energy would be directed at training his successors so they're able to grasp the baton he's offering and carry on the race.

He does some of this, of course, but far from everything possible. He's too busy doing other things, such as enjoying himself, taking out what he put in through all those lean years, maintaining his own security, and (more important, perhaps, than everything else) making sure he has something to do with himself.

In some senses, he may be doing what he's doing to be *with* the kids. He probably feels some guilt for not spending enough time with them when they were very young, and leaving the whole thing to Mom while he worked the farm. Now, much later, the operation can provide him with a chance to spend time with the kids without sacrificing his attention to the farm.

No. Dad's not doing it all for the kids' benefit.

Nor should he be.

WHY # 2: *"Everybody Deserves a Chance To Benefit."*

Partially, this is a "being your own boss" justification for family farm continuity. Part of it involves the legacy concept — why else did we build this farm, if not to use it to take advantage of independence and all the good aspects of the American Dream?

Yes, the benefits are very easy to get used to. There's the opportunity to work for yourself, the opportunity to control your own destiny (sort of), and the chance to be financially secure (sort of).

For successors, of course, these "benefits" are "later" rather than "now" — they only come when and after Dad lets go of the helm.

Well, the benefits are important, sure, but control and freedom are *future* benefits; they don't explain why so many heirs stay with their family companies waiting for those good things to arrive.

WHY # 3: *"It's the Best Opportunity Available."*

If this statement is true, great. Too often, however, this isn't really what's being said. Too often, the family farm is the *only*, not necessarily the *best*, opportunity available.

The sentiment can be expressed in a number of ways. We've heard heirs speak openly of their family farms as "safe harbors," and admit they felt that what they knew was preferable to what they didn't know.

These are the statements of prisoners, someone locked

in place because of a lack of options. The bars don't have to be obvious. One can be as easily imprisoned by inertia, the love of security, or comfort, as by the "hardware" of family farm imprisonment: golden handcuffs, lack of outside experience, inadequate training, advanced age.

However the doors are locked, they're locked. That's a heck of a reason to decide you *want* to stay around.

A truly beneficial family farm will expand the range of options available, not eliminate the need for options.

WHY #4: *"There's Too Much Time (Money) Invested To Quit Now."*

Another way of saying this is: "Just be patient. It'll All Work Out."

Problem is, it won't "work out," not unless we do something to make things happen. Instead of soothing the pain, blind hope almost guarantees it will only get worse.

WHY #5: *"It's What My Spouse Wants."*

By its nature, a family farm is a family affair. It's more than just a career for the family managers. It's also a "career" for their spouses and their children. The family farm lives with everyone, it's a large part of their waking activities, a lot of their dreams, and far too many of their nightmares.

Both spouses "gotta wanna." To put aside cherished personal goals so the spouse can work the farm is to ask for trouble later (and maybe not that much later).

"Do what you think best," all too readily evolves into "Do what you want, but don't expect me to believe in it (or like it)."

WHY #6: *"It's Important to the Family."*

This "why" takes many forms. Here are just a few:

- *Dad couldn't make it without me/us.*

- *My sister, or my brother, or Mom (etc.) needs me to manage the farm and keep the investment safe.*

> • *It would really hurt my brother (father, etc.) if I left.*

They each sound good, but they ignore the truly important issue. What's important to the family is to be able to stay together in love, trust and respect. As long as the farm helps this to happen, continuity of the operation is important to the family. If, on the other hand, the farm is becoming a source of dislike, distrust and disrespect, fighting to keep it for the sake of the family is to fight for the right to commit "familicide."

WHY #7: *"It's Something Dad (and Granddad and Great-Granddad . . .) Always Wanted."*
This we hear expressed in different ways:

> • *"This is what Dad wants for us."*
>
> • *"Dad expects us to stay."*

However it's said, it expresses a sense of "imprisonment," as though a burden of guilt and responsibility was placed on the heirs' shoulders by Mom and Dad, and the heirs reluctantly go along.

True, Dad might want the family to work together in a successful growing operation that he built. But other questions need to be asked. Is this what's going to happen if the family stays in farming? Will the family, indeed, be able to work *together?*

Parents readily deny these motives, openly stating that to work on the farm because "Mom and Dad want it" is definitely the wrong reason for staying. Our statistics are unofficial, but far fewer parents seem to want to force their kids into farming than the "captured" heirs seem to think.

Rather than serving as a primary reason, "It's Something Dad Always Wanted,"is better viewed as a side benefit of owning a family farm that's held together for other reasons that are more sound.

WHY #8: *"There's Always the Chance It'll Be Worth More Someday."*

And there's always the chance that it won't.

A successful, growing family farm can be a good investment, but generally only for on-farm owners. Minority ownership by off-farm heirs is a plain lousy investment, even if the operation is growing and successful. The assets are illiquid, it pays few, if any, dividends, and there's no market for the heirs' interest or share.

Is this the kind of investment that would justify the family conflicts "mixed" ownership can bring?

Even for the on-farm owners, who have more opportunities to benefit from their ownership through salaries, benefits, and the like, the cash portion of their return can often be lower than they'd get from other investments.

Farm ownership offers intangible returns — personal control, fun, life style, challenge, opportunity — which must be figured into total return. If those intangibles aren't there, if the farm isn't fun and the family isn't getting along, overall return can be very low indeed.

To stick with it for some undefined, possible future return when today's return is inadequate is to ignore reality and believe, instead, in Shangri-La.

WHY # 9: *"We've Got To Protect Our Rights — and the Rights of Our Kids."*

Rights? To what? Not to asset value — the farm belongs to the present owners and they can do what they want with what they own. There are no moral "rights" to an inheritance.

To jobs and salaries? To have it all? To have as much as everybody else? These aren't "rights." They're possibilities, opportunities, gifts — all of which are matters of good fortune, hard work, and commitment that can easily be destroyed by unjustified demands.

This isn't a reason for sticking it out on a family farm. It's a cause of conflict and the eventual destruction of everything good and true within that farm business.

In short, many of the reasons commonly given for sticking with a family farm might sound good, but they generally don't hold water.

While we can criticize many of the above reasons for fighting the family farm fight, there's little question that they are used by many people. Unfortunately, these "wrong" reasons are the causes of many of the frustrations and conflicts that occur on family farms.

By now it should be fairly clear that family farms aren't held together because of their shining qualities as investments. The investment factor is, and always will be, important, of course, but it seldom seems paramount in the minds of family farm owners.

Something else, more powerful and persuasive, seems to operate on the best of family farms: the potential that farm ownership offers to expand the best parts of family life.

This is the fundamental "why," at any rate it's the one that operates in the most successful families in farming. And if we can accept the validity of family togetherness as a reason to stay in business together, then we must also accept the challenge to manage that operation and the family in a way that will ensure "togetherness" is achieved.

The negative aspects of the family farm should never be accepted as inevitable, unavoidable, and incurable. Once, and if, they are, we've lost the basic reason for staying involved at all.

For successful families, the family farm helps solve family problems — and helps keep them solved. Keeping the farm in the family is a way to develop closeness and openness in communication, even though it might not have existed previously in the family.

These are the positive reasons for staying together as a family in farming, not in theory, but in fact. Most, if not all of these benefits are experienced by the families that have been successful at bringing different generations together for continuity and success.

Chapter 10
HOW HEIRS CHANGE AS THE YEARS GO BY

Typically, in a farm with second-generation management (usually run by brothers, but, obviously, variations are possible), the operating style is relatively informal and cooperative. Each second-generation manager finds his or her own strengths and abilities, and directs activities in those directions. This isn't quite the way Grandpa did things, but it works nevertheless.

Great. This is usually what the present generation takes for granted — and it's what they build into their estate planning.

Again, great. Great, that is, if the following generations of heirs will be just like us.

Trouble is, they won't. They can't. And we've got to plan for the differences, or we have trouble on the farm.

COUSINS ARE DIFFERENT

With the arrival of following generations, new problems arise:

1) **Heirs have greater freedom in career choice.**

111

There is at least an equal chance that third (and following) generation heirs will decide on careers outside the family farm. This raises complications because it usually sets up a potential conflict between the managing and off-farm cousins and siblings.

Off-farm heirs typically don't get involved in management. They're more like absentee land owners, capable of complaining, capable of siding with Mom or a sister. Off-farm heirs, for many reasons that aren't even their fault, are in a position to cause a lot of trouble. They don't even have enough information to provide constructive ideas or realistic support.

This situation, in fact, is what makes the next generation as secretive as Dad. Only their reasons are different. We've developed an axiom of agriculture: When you have non-farm minority owners involved in your farm business, the "family reunion" is almost guaranteed to turn into a "family revolution."

2) Management decisions move from the hands of a very few, into the hands of a widening "bureaucracy."

The latter-generation farm operator — family or non-family — has many people to please, and usually he finds very little agreement or consensus among that crowd as to what makes a good decision.

What does this do? It ties his hands and limits his ability to follow a steady course. It, effectively, turns him into a bureaucrat, too.

3) Income ceases to be a major issue for the owners, who yield instead to concerns about asset management and tax planning.

If a farm has survived long enough to be successful with third- and subsequent generations of heirs, we can assume a certain amount of wealth . Successful farms are prosperous. But given this, we have to consider what change that "wealth" will bring to the outlooks of the owners.

Difficult as "relative compensation" *(who's gettin' paid*

what, and why aren't I?) issues can be, latter-generation heirs find themselves very much tied together and, therefore, inflexible in managing their joint assets.

4) **Concerns for getting things going and making things work yield to concerns for keeping things going.**

The "old days" where a good operator or a brilliant farmer could save the day eventually fade into wistful memories. Now, so much more is involved. There's income to think about, and owners' rights, and all kinds of things that have nothing to do with the day-to-day operation of the farm.

Often, the heir or heirs who choose to stay on the farm really want to stay. They can go to unbelievable extremes to make that succession happen. Typically, the off-farm heirs are supportive, for a while. They know that Dad wanted to see the farm continue, and that's their wish, too — until reality begins to set in. That happens when they learn that they can't have any benefit from their inheritance as long as it's operated by the on-farm heir. At this point, Dad's wishes and the on-farm heir's hopes get set aside and the non-farm heirs begin to think seriously about selling the operation.

> *"I mean, can Cousin Charlie really run the place?" "What exactly are we getting for all that money tied up in dirt?"*

Good questions, all, but difficult to answer in a way that satisfies off-farm heirs as well as on-farm heirs. In the typical in-town family business, these factions become opposing shareholders voting their individual percentages. Not so on most family farms, where "shareholder" influence is more likely to be based on personal influence and relationships. The stronger and more influential the off-farm heirs in personality, the cloudier is the future of the farm.

Some of the options usually thought of first (like sale or possible development) by third- and fourth-generation heirs would have been blasphemy to Granddad and, often, to his successors. With the passage of time, however, they increasingly demand consideration.

5) **The owners' relationships to each other become more emotionally distant.**

In almost any family, the emotional closeness among cousins decreases with the passage of time. The fact that these cousins might share ownership in a successful farm doesn't seem to help. The wider ownership simply becomes less focused than it was in the preceding generation.

In the typical family, this isn't mourned, except maybe by the older folks who remember the big family holiday gatherings which are long passed. But in a family that owns a farm, it must be considered. Emotional distance between owners generates an increasing explosiveness in family farm discussions.

6) **The new "Boss" of a third-generation family farm can be truly effective only under one of two circumstances:**

a) He is able to function as a powerful, respected "head of the clan," or

b) He is able to operate under a charter given to him by the family in the form of shared family goals.

Disappearing forever in the third-generation farm is the day of the self-defined patriarch (or matriarch).

NON-FAMILY MANAGERS ARE DIFFERENT, TOO

As time goes by, it also becomes more likely that non-family managers, a rare but growing breed, will be brought onto the farm. They bring a lot of differences with them, too — particularly if they're eventually going to own the place.

In farm operations with non-family successors, return on investment is very likely to become very important for both the present and the future owner — something that's not always true with family successors. Other non-family managers who aren't, and never were, slated for ownership are likely to expect some "return" on their "investment," too.

The likelihood that an owner and the non-family successors will share dreams and values is very slim, although it does happen. Certainly, where dreams and values *are* shared, the owners, the non-family successor(s), and the non-family managers have an advantage. But, even here, it's dangerous to assume that these shared values are enough to ensure the process will stick to the end.

Dad and his non-family managers should at least discuss the issues, and settle, openly and frankly, their "whys" as early as possible in their relationship. The bitter experiences of too many have underlined, again and again, the importance of reaching this understanding.

The "whys" are important — for everybody involved in a family farm. They determine how the company is managed. They determine the goals that are set. And they set the tone, the atmosphere under which everybody operates.

At bottom, when a non-family successor is going to be chosen, the goal of succession planning is setting up an organization that can help family members as well as non-family managers get the benefits of farm ownership.

DIFFERENT PLANS FOR LATER GENERATIONS

What today's farm owner decides about passing on the farm has an impact on the entire future of that farm. He or she must, therefore, think about more than just the next generation — his children and/or his successors.

Some thought has to be given to the needs and concerns of subsequent generations, because, for them, things are going to be different from what they are today.

The most basic change in perspective occurs between the second and third generation of ownership. After that, the changes are a matter of degree. So, for simplicity, we'll just look at the second-to-third generation differences here:

1) **Co-Owners will be very different in personal goals, lifestyles, and values.**

Many of these differences exist among brothers and sisters in the first and second generations, but in the third and following generations, many of the heirs are likely to be *cousins* (or even more distant in relationship).

As new generations come along, shared experiences tend to get thinner, while individual differences multiply. This isn't necessarily a weakness or a problem. It can, in fact, add strength and vitality through diversity. But the less we've done together, the more likely we are to misunderstand each other — and herein lies the root of many latter-generation family problems.

Given this, planning for the future should include planning for handling — and settling — disagreement among the owners.

2) Misunderstandings and disagreements among the owners are much more difficult to handle.

This is why managing disagreement must be planned for in future generations. It's not that the earlier owners always got along perfectly, but that they had more reason/ability to settle their problems in a friendly way.

While, in most cases, third generation shareholder disagreements aren't necessarily more sticky than disagreements in the first or second generations, there *are* a lot more of them. This simple fact of life, in effect, makes agreement more difficult to achieve from the inside.

Thus, the present owner should also plan to meet the increasing need for outside influence to maintain agreement among his heirs.

3) Relatively fewer heirs have the desire to become operators of the farm.

This is typical among third (and subsequent) generation heirs, and the reasons should be obvious.

With expanding ownership, there is an expanding emotional gap between the farm operation and the potential heirs. The family farm is no longer by definition the major factor in the heir's future, and, in fact, not all heirs can be accommodated. In short, working on the family farm is no longer the given career route for heirs in future generations.

The problem (as we stated earlier) is multiplied by the fact that farms don't generate levels of income anything like one would expect from the level of assets. This leads, often, to a struggle between the few who have remained with the operation, and the many who would like to get some "benefit" from their inheritance.

Often, both groups feel frustrated. One is frustrated by being unable to buy out or provide a reasonable return to the off-farm relatives. The off-farm heirs feel frustrated because, down deep, they know Mom and Dad or Granddad wanted them to get something out of it, too.

Thus, estate and management transition planning must take into account the increasing possibility of off-farm heirs in following generations. In order to maintain the farm as an economical, viable, producing unit, estate and succession techniques must be used to solidify the ownership in the hands of the farmers, and yet provide a means whereby the non-farmers can get their benefit, too. And all this must be done in a way that doesn't hamstring or smother the farm operation.

Quite a trick . . . but it usually can be done.

4) There is a decreasing likelihood that all heirs will agree with the family "philosophy."

This is the farm's "culture," and as the number of heirs increases and they grow more distant from each other, we can no longer take for granted that family members will see the farm in a single, unified way.

Instead of feeling a commitment to the land, for example, some heirs might feel that real estate development is the best use of family assets. The real estate numbers will simply be more persuasive for someone less emotionally attached to the farm than were their predecessors.

Despite what the on-farm successor(s) may think, there's nothing inherently right about a given "culture." Consequently, today's farm owner makes a mistake when he or she assumes that the basic family values will (or even should) be shared by all future generations, and then bases his plans on that assumption.

5) **There will probably be less agreement that the farm should stay under family ownership.**

Dad almost guarantees very basic disagreement by setting up a whole mess of off-farm heirs through his estate. Farm ownership by off-farm heirs, attractive as it might sound, is sure not what it's cracked up to be. This is why non-farm heirs tend to be a major source of rumblings about sale, particularly in family farms passed down in such a way that off-farm heirs can't get income.

If the farm is out in the middle of the Great Plains, and there are no alternative uses for the land, the off-farm heirs will have to be satisfied with whatever rent they can negotiate with their farmer-relatives. But if the farm is near a city, for example, and the land could be sold for $5000 an acre, the picture is entirely different.

We have a client whose operation is next to a municipal golf course. The male cousins are working together. The female cousins, who outnumber them, aren't interested in the business. The boys' greatest fear is that the girls will inherit the land in such a way that could force a sale. The prospect for these off-farm heirs would be tempting, given the possibility the land could go for $5000 an acre.

This kind of time-bomb must be avoided through planning. Estate and transition plans, in general, should either provide some form of affordable and fair liquidity for off-farm heirs — or those plans should avoid creating off-farm owners in the first place.

The Boss, in short, can't be content to plan the transition only to his immediate heirs. He — and his advisors — also have to give thought to how the immediate succession plan will effect following generations of heirs. Presumably, The Boss is planning for *continuity*, not only tax savings or a short-term emotional truce. This is a large responsibility.

The question facing every farm owner is how to go about assuring that the farm will continue to grow and prosper as a successful family-owned operation. For that to happen, his goal for the future has to be achieving and maintaining fundamental agreement among the heirs — *today and tomorrow.*

If any plan is going to work, we can't destroy the possibility of agreement among the heirs. Of course, we can't ever expect *complete* agreement among them — intelligent, capable people inevitably have independent and unique personalities, but there must be a clear and unambiguous plan that takes care of the needs of on-farm and off-farm heirs alike. If we can accomplish this, while allowing the present owner protection and flexibility, we've found the fundamental key to successful estate planning.

Chapter 11
WHY IT'S SO TOUGH TO "GIVE IT ALL AWAY"

We could spend volumes clucking over almost infinite variations on the failure-to-do-estate planning horror story, but we don't have volumes at our disposal. Nevertheless, some "f'rinstances" might be useful, if only to demonstrate the horrendous ramifications of simply doing nothing.

Founders build businesses and farms. Successors develop them and keep them alive. That's something we all know. Something many of us *don't* realize, however, is that the successful farmer and his family often have parallel skills at *demolition*.

All the while they're building a successful farm operation, they're laying booby traps and detonators under the barn floor. These time bombs might take a long time to go off — but go off they do.

THE REQUIRED "HORROR STORY"

An example of a company on the West Coast comes to mind. This is a farm implement dealership that's now in its fourth generation of family management. A success story on the surface, this company is now showing the spreading cracks from explosions among the family's underground bombs.

And there seem to be more to come.

The company was founded as a blacksmith shop at the turn of the century and now has a sales volume in excess of $10 million. The president of the company (we'll call him "Bill") works in the business with his brother. They're great-grandsons of the founder. Neither of them has any ownership — what their branch of the family owns, 25% of the stock, is in the hands of their mother. The rest sits in 12.5% blocks in the hands of the founder's six other great grandchildren.

We'll get to the "cracks" in a moment, but first you should have an understanding of how this interesting ownership distribution came about. Great-granddad had two sons, both of whom worked for him and who, quite naturally, divided the ownership of the business after the old blacksmith's demise.

To this point, it's a typical family agri-business story. Nothing all that unusual, until, about 10 years after the founder died, the two second-generation heirs (Bill's grandfather and grand-uncle) got into a conflict of some sort (nobody today remembers what it was about), which resulted in Bill's grand-uncle walking out of the business — taking his 50% along.

As a consequence, the ownership of this company is now divided equally among involved and non-involved families. Within living memory, it's never been any other way.

The departure of that 50% block of ownership with Bill's grand-uncle thickened the plot considerably. That wayward 50% went to an only son, who not long ago divided his shares among four daughters. Bill's grandfather left the half that stayed with the company to Bill's father and Bill's uncle, both of whom worked in the company all their lives. Bill's father then left his shares to his wife, Bill's mother. The uncle's 25% went to two sons who work in the company with Bill.

You may be having a hard time following all this, but you can bet the owners aren't. They think about it all the time.

All the time.

Bill and his brother thought it was okay for their mother to have the stock — until Mom and her daughters-in-law stopped getting along with each other. Miffed and resentful, Mom is presently alternating between threats to put it all in trust for charity and hints of a long-term "liaison" with a retired attorney in Ft. Myers. Bill's uncle is still on the board, but disabled by a major stroke.

The four "wayward" shareholder-daughters and Bill's Mom are lobbying for larger dividends. Bill thinks the company should expand. The two ideas are not complementary, and they're definitely not compatible.

Even though Bill has done a great job as the fourth-generation president, his attention and his energy are increasingly concentrated elsewhere. His main worry is not how to be successful, but rather whether he's foolish to build a successful company under the thumb of his shareholder relatives. A few well-formed alliances among the disgruntled, after all, could easily push him out the door.

So much for a well-planned estate.

Another example of the sorry condition of estate planning on the American family farm concerns a young man we met at a convention in the Northwest. His father had started their family Christmas tree operation, had given 5% ownership to each of two key employees, and planned on passing the operation on to his son eventually.

It didn't happen that way, unfortunately. Dad died "prematurely," before he could get around to changing the share repurchase agreement, and the 10% in non-family hands suddenly became 100% in non-family hands. This is called agricultural disinheritance by accident.

So much for a timely estate plan.

WHY ESTATE PLANS DON'T GET DONE

Why do otherwise intelligent human beings so often allow their major asset to bounce around helplessly on the wheel of chance? From what we've seen, it's only for the best of reasons.

Precisely because they want to do the right thing, successful farm owners fail, absolutely, to do anything at all.

Almost without fail, whenever we ask an audience of farm owners for a show of hands by those who have a viable, up-to-date estate plan, only five to 10 percent will raise their hands. When we ask, further, how many of *them* have discussed that plan with their heirs, most of those few hands drop quickly.

This almost universal failure is easily understood. In the first place, it's tough talking about estate planning. If Dad brings it up to Mom and the kids, he figures they'll think he's a candidate for open heart surgery. If Mom asks him, he'll probably start wondering if she's really going to the sewing group those afternoons she's "out." And the kids — the only reason they'd ask is because they were broke or itching to get their hands on his money.

So who brings it up? Nobody — except Dad's insurance agent or maybe the lawyer — and they have their own motives, too. Right?

There's more than simple discomfort involved, though. There's also a lot of doubt in Dad's mind about what's the best thing to do. When he looks at his heirs, he often sees their anxiety and disagreements. He sees their tugging at the traces, longing for "freedom," and wonders if he shouldn't just liquidate and let them loose. But his whole history and background — and his hope — cry against such a solution.

> *"Someday,"* as a Mexican vegetable grower
> once said to us, *"they will come to their senses and
> see what it means to have a place to work."*

Dad hopes that time and more success will solve the confusions within his family. Faced with these two extremes — sale or delay — he almost inevitably chooses to wait.

There'll be some pressure from his advisors if they're worth their fees, but he's not easy to move. *"Gee, Joe,"* they probably said to him a few years back, *"you really ought to do something about your estate."* He agreed. Of course. It's just that he never got around to it.

And he's not unique. There surely are hundreds of thousands of carefully constructed estate plans lying around farm owners' desks, dusty and *unsigned*.

They'll get around to *those* someday, too.

Sure they will — posthumously. The farm owner's desires too often pass on with him, leaving his advisors to hammer out hasty damage control measures over cold coffee and assorted cold cuts at The Boss's funeral breakfast.

DAD'S REASONS FOR WAITING

Why doesn't the farm owner plan his or her estate? It's not really to be contrary or to cause problems for the next generation. That might be the effect of inaction, but usually it's not his real intent. Usually a number of other problems lead him to say "later" to acting on his plan for passing down the farm:

1) **The Desire To Be "Fair."**

Farm owners, like most human parents, love their children equally and have equivalent concerns for the welfare of each. So, when it comes to thinking about an estate plan that's "fair," they tend to think in terms of "equal." Why else would there be so many second-generation family farms owned in equal parts by involved and non-involved siblings?

But is "equal" really "fair"? Here's how it works: Joe owns half, does all the work, and gets to take out all the money. Sister Kate owns half, lives a thousand miles away, does none of the work, and takes out no money. Guess who becomes a thorn in whose side — and who feels the other is unfairly sharing in whose hard-won equity growth? They both do, of course.

What about the on-farm heir who worked for Dad for 20 years? During that time, the money he would have made in any other business went into tilling the land, buying irrigation equipment, planting asparagus, fruit trees, and other perennials — all aimed at making the farm grow. The strategy succeeded, and now the value of the land has increased dramatically. Now all he has to do is buy it all back again from his off-farm brothers and sisters!

Is it "fair" to spend half of your life sacrificing and building up the family's farm business just to have the "pleasure" of buying back the part of it that was left to the off-farm heirs (who, by the way, have been making a good income in "real jobs" in town)?

Sometimes "fair" is defined as leaving the farm to Mother. Let her decide — at least we've made sure the kids will be nice to her in her fading years. The way this "works" is: rotating authority, hobbled successor-managers, and insecure widows who control farms rather than money.

Having Mom as the controlling owner scares most thoughtful heirs, just as depending for her security on her kids scares Mom. During the years when they should be growing and expanding and investing, she's justifiably afraid of any decisions that put her security in danger. Also, the off-farm heirs can be putting subtle pressure on her, and, out of love, she takes the "one-share-per-kid" route, almost guaranteeing the problems described earlier.

"Fair" can be achieved in lots of creative, if irrational, ways — usually involving some variation on this "equality" theme. However, the concern for evenhandedness, amplified by emotion and love, too often overwhelms the whispered advice of logic and business sense.

But don't think this fair/equal dilemma is lost on Dad. After all, he didn't get where he is by being stupid or insensitive. No, he often sees all too clearly that there's a major conflict between what's good for his family and what's good for the farm.

He can opt for one or the other out of sheer exhaustion, or he can decide to wait. Maybe something will come up to clarify matters.

Maybe.

2) **Doubts about the Successors.**

(Or, as a corollary, their doubts about Dad.) How can the farm owner decide how — not to mention when — to pass on management and control of his operation when the real leader (read "Dad's Clone") hasn't emerged, or the youngsters aren't ready, or they don't get along, or he doesn't trust that guy his daughter married?

How can he decide to give up control of his farm when Junior keeps buying antique tractors, or investing in the Mexican Peso, or rehearsing his rock group?

> *"I know we've always put money in the bank, Dad, but computer software is where it's at today. That's the business we should invest in."*

How's Dad supposed to decide under those conditions? He's not. And he won't. Period.

We've seen farm owners stand firm on their inaction, year after year, bending nary a little under the gale of dire warnings from advisors and successors about "liquidity problems," the predictable disasters that are going to happen when Uncle Sam's goon squads descend on the disorganized, freshly opened estate.

> *"The farm is going to go under, Dad!"*

> *"Says who?"* he asks, his mind working, thinking: *Besides, maybe there wouldn't be such a problem if you sold that sports car of yours and put the money in the farm.*

When there's a problem, Dad knows it, but sometimes in his weaker moments he wonders if maybe it isn't *his* problem. Instead, maybe if things go sour, it's *somebody else's* just deserts — the Lord's way of righting a wrong, so to speak.

But those weak moments don't last. He wants to see the farm continue, but doesn't know what to do. We've seen farmers, year after year, pushing aside sound estate advice because they "want to see what (or whether) Junior decides to do" or they "need more time to observe the two of them," "can't see a daughter working a farm," or "want to be sure that guy isn't going to walk out on my daughter — divorce isn't just in town anymore."

Most other professional advisors have seen it, too, much to their frustration. Old Dad just won't move.

But, then, would *you*, under the same circumstances?

3) **An Overdeveloped Sense of Longevity.**

We had a client who, after a serious heart attack and a quadruple bypass, finally decided there was a possibility he wouldn't live forever.

Well, when it happens, each of us will be convinced we died prematurely. It's only others who so generously reflect that "He had a full life."

For many reasons, the family farmer is more prone to this sort of assumed immortality than most lesser humans. He's *always* been busy. He's *always* been healthy. He's *always* worked hard. He's a *survivor*. It's almost impossible for him to imagine anything different.

Often, the farm owner's procrastination is due in part (if not in total) to his unwavering conviction that there's always time to get it done, plenty of time. Estate planning just doesn't seem all that urgent, especially not with all the business problems he has to solve *today*. Hell, if we don't survive this recession, what good's an estate plan going to do?

He'll do it "later," and there's always going to be a later.

4) **"My operation is different."**

Nobody really understands Dad's problems, see? There may be answers for other farms, Dad often thinks, and, sure, there may be a few smart lawyers and people like that out there — but none of that really applies to me. His situation is so complex that 10 years of worry and thought on his part haven't even begun to unravel a solution. How is some uninformed advisor or consultant going to do it (even if they are smart)?

If his business were, in fact, that different, then his conclusions would be justified. But this book, by itself, should be enough evidence of how *undifferent* most family farms are from each other — a fortunate fact, actually, at least for estate planning purposes.

Lord, if every operation were so different, there would be *no* answers. Imagine, for example, what the world of medicine would be like if every human body were different — different organs, tissues, blood. With every sickness, the entire body of medical knowledge would have to be rediscovered. Health care would be hokus pokus, mostly self-delivered. It would be a world in which you would sue *yourself* for malpractice.

No, we should be thankful we aren't all that unique. While it's true that family farms *are* different from each other in many ways, the differences aren't quantum leaps. They are variations on some fairly well-understood themes, and there's precedent for most every situation.

Over the centuries, a body of law and practice has accumulated that is flexible enough to handle almost every problem, no matter how complex or unique the problems might seem to the people involved.

Unfortunately, too few farm owners accept the possibility that somebody else might have the answers to questions they've been asking themselves for years. Instead, they draw the blinds even tighter and withdraw into their own worries. They consult the only oracle they know — themselves — and the answer, almost invariably, is "we're workin' on it."

Farm owners aren't the only people alone with their internal prophets. Their heirs go through a lot of temple haunting of their own, although with one very important difference. The heirs actually go out and *look* for ideas.

Most of the time, however, they limit their search to books and specialized seminars. They want to do it themselves, partially because they have no greater love for paying professional fees than Dad does, but partially, too, because they have a suspicion that the solution they would like to see is not the solution an objective outsider would consider right or fair, much less practical or feasible.

So to Dad's theme, "My *operation* is different," the heirs compose a new refrain: "My *problem* is different.

We've gone through long exploratory discussions with heirs about succession planning in their family businesses, only to find that the answer they're seeking involves some form of financial assassination of other family members.

Succession planning is fine as far as it goes, they admit, but theirs is a different situation. No one (they say) understands how much the success of the farm is due to their efforts alone, and what a drain their brothers — or sisters — are . . . And on it goes.

Dad, of course, sees the smoke rising out of this silent, underground war, and it bothers him greatly. If they can't get along now, what happen's after I'm gone? See, he protests, my business *is* different. Look at all the problems I have. How can anybody else's solution work with this family?

Well, no specific individual's solution can work, most likely, but there are approaches that can work to everyone's benefit.

One thing sure, waiting for things to become more clear, or waiting for a sign from heaven, is very dangerous. That lightning seldom strikes.

No, the key lies in defining what basic outcome seems best, then finding the tools to get it done.

And the first step is getting the priorities of estate planning in good, solid order.

Chapter 12
THE 4 PILLARS OF ESTATE PLANNING

As the old saying goes, if you don't change the way you're headed, you'll end up where you're going. The saying fits estate planning real well.

Sure, most family farms have some sort of plan for the estate and the future. It's hard to avoid such planning totally. But it's seldom enough to have a few technical devices in place — as far too many families find out after death kicks some of these devices into play.

Too often, the "answers" farm owners come up with for their estates were pasted together over time — different answers for specific problems as they arose, with little consideration given to how all these jigsaw pieces were to fit together to solve the big puzzle. And if that isn't bad enough, when Dad doesn't confront the problems, he comes up with watered down compromises that don't really benefit anybody.

Too often, what little estate planning Dad does (fortunate as it might be that he did any at all), he does chasing only one or two independent and unrelated goals. The big picture is usually ignored, leading to some critical faults in his plan.

The big picture should get a lot more respect. Planning the ownership and management transition of a family farm is a complex process that rates a lot more attention than it gets. But, in other senses, farm owners see the process as more complex than it needs to be — probably one of the major reasons they don't usually get it done. Major Reason # 2 is the fact that Dad doesn't trust anyone enough to tell them enough so they can help him.

A FADING FAD?

During the 70's, every farm publication in existence spent page after page dealing with topics related to estate planning and the family farm. They talked about rising land values and confiscatory estate taxes. There were horror stories of family farms being lost. They wrote success stories about how this or that family "did it."

Most farmers read all these articles. They even kept files on them. We saw it over and over. A client would get up in the middle of a conversation, walk over to the file cabinet, and pull out a file folder full of articles on one estate planning topic or another.

The farmer's concern about the future wasn't an idle curiosity. The most important goal of most family farmers is to have the farm continue on, in their family, into the next generation. They heard about all the problems with taxes and all that, and they got concerned about estate planning.

But today, "estate planning" seems out of fashion as a topic of interest. In today's economic climate, particularly with the tax act of 1981 which "reduced" estate taxes, and with the turnaround in land values, estate planning articles and seminars have virtually disappeared.

The whole movement toward estate planning in agriculture seemed motivated by a fear of spiraling inflation, the fear of increasing land values, and a tax system that was seen as just plain robbery.

Well, today it's different, right? Land values have gone

down. Tax laws have changed. True. But do these changes really mean that estate planning is no longer needed?

The fact is, land values *have* gone down, but, actually, the tax laws haven't really been changed very much. Sure, they raised the threshold so that more people are able to avoid taxes altogether, but there are a lot of asset-rich farmers out there who will end up paying more than they expect, even after tax "reform." They'll pay more because they didn't plan.

We see an entirely different aspect of the estate planning problem, probably because we find so many farms involved in estate "damage control" — trying to minimize the disaster that results from an unplanned estate.

Sure, there was a lot of interest and concern about estate planning back in the late 70's, but even then there was little of it done. Now, we have a few positive reforms which bring relief — and make it even less likely that successful farmers will do the estate planning they should be doing.

Well, there's no reason why we should accept the failure to plan as inevitable — and a lot of really powerful reasons why we shouldn't.

Fact is, estate planning isn't magic, or voodoo, or a secret ritual reserved for experts. It's a basically understandable process of discovering and coordinating needs and objectives. It is also one that inevitably requires expert help to put together. Still, the fundamentals are understandable by any reasonably intelligent individual — and they must be understood, because no expert, alone, can define a family's goals and needs. He can only *help* identify and reach them.

TAXES AREN'T EVERYTHING

In estate planning for the family farm, there are two important issues that must be addressed: shifting ownership and control, and avoiding unnecessary taxes. The former is most critical to the long-term health of the farm operation and the family. The latter, tax avoidance, has a short-term importance only, but it often absorbs the most planning energy — and causes the most plans to go awry, long-term.

The goal of family farm estate planning is most often *continuity*, not the saving of taxes nor even the manipulation of power. While the purity of motives might change as future generations get involved with the operation, continuity is usually the goal of the present owner as he does his crystal ball gazing at his potential heirs.

Since his plan usually sets the tone for the future, the quality of that initial plan has a lot to do with what future generations do.

So it's essential to look at much more than taxes.

Actually, there are four pillars supporting every good estate plan, and they each have to carry their part of the weight. If any one is missing or inadequate or over-built, the plan is almost guaranteed to be unstable, unlivable, and short-lived.

PILLAR #1: DECIDING WHO'S GOING TO RUN THE FARM.

The plan must, first of all, take survival of the farm into account. To be successful, a family farm must have capable, committed, knowledgeable operating managers. "Managers" is a word we chose deliberately, because tomorrow's farmer must be a manager first, a farmer second.

Provision for management succession has to be considered as part of the process of deciding where ownership and control are going to be placed. Who will the key managers be after Dad retires or dies? When will this passing of the baton take place and how will it be done?

A realistic look has to be taken at the abilities of the potential family successors, and those abilities should be compared to the abilities of the key non-family managers.

PILLAR #2: DECIDING WHO'S GOING TO OWN WHAT.

Ownership and management have to be transferred in a way that minimizes the potential for conflict among future generations. A glance at the problems facing Bill and his family in their farm implement dealership (see the previous chapter) presents a fairly distressing picture of what can happen when equity is distributed without forethought.

The problem of how to give it away "fairly" is a most agonizing one for the farm owner. He typically sees his farm as a "legacy" for his children, and, quite naturally, he feels a legacy is something his heirs (all of them) should benefit from forever. So . . . they should all benefit from the farm forever. He thereby confuses ownership with benefit — a confusion most off-farm heirs clear up for themselves very early, and very painfully.

In Bill's dealership, for example, the major conflict between the owning families is a disagreement whether to distribute profits or reinvest for growth. Unfortunately, one option tends to exclude the other.

Quite naturally, Bill would like to see expansion. That solidifies his place in the company — and, besides, he's already taking his "profits" out in the form of salary. But the stability of those benefits is very fragile for him because he has no control over the business. The operational rug can be yanked at any time.

His non-involved shareholder relatives don't get a salary and have very few "bennies." They own a significant portion of a sizable operation, yet, for them, there is no "benefit" at all — unless large dividends are paid, something that would turn the company into a cash (and dying?) cow.

Is this the kind of legacy Great Granddad really had in mind for his heirs?

Hardly. But this problem, or problems like it, are almost inevitable if we don't think through what we want to accomplish. Advisors can't do this for us; they can only help. We have to do it for ourselves, being very careful to distinguish between the wealth that can come from sale and the opportunity for a successful life in farming.

Wealth *is* opportunity, sure, but it's an undefined opportunity without a "base of operation." Opportunity of the kind represented by a successful family farm, on the other hand, is a defined possibility which begins from a significant base: the successful operation.

This is a helpful distinction, because it means Dad doesn't have to leave *opportunity* to everybody. In fact, he should leave it only to those who want and can make use of it. It's not sensible to expect those who've chosen a non-farm life style to want anything other than the money that is represented by their share of the inheritance. On the other hand, "opportunity" for the on-farm people is the chance to farm.

His decision boils down to two questions:

a) *Should off-farm family members share in the equity growth resulting from the work and talent of the family managers?* In most cases, especially where continuity rather than sale of the farm is really the major goal, they shouldn't. To give them such benefit can remove any incentive for the family managers to manage for growth.

b) *Should on-farm heirs be in a position to take salaries and perks while off-farm heirs receive only paper growth?* This hardly seems like equality of ownership and opportunity?

The on-farm heir earns his income mostly through his physical efforts, which the off-farm heirs don't share. So salary shouldn't be an issue — everybody expects to get paid for what they do. But the on-farm heir also gets profits. He gets tax benefits, depreciation, a house to live in, free gas, and the freedom of being his own boss. This balances the risk he takes, of course, but off-farm owners get none of these things. In essence, they get nothing but the vague promise of possible wealth sometime in the distant future.

We wonder why off-farm heirs get disgruntled?

Few people outside of agriculture understand that the family farm has very little "going concern" value, primarily because of the way crops are marketed. Some do, but most don't. So the option left to family operators is usually a matter of auctioning off parcels of land to the neighbors, selling the silos and hauling them down the road, maybe keeping the homestead for one of the kids.

The family farm isn't like the in-town automobile dealership which can be sold to the next guy as a viable business. The value of the farm to others is the value of the underlying assets. To the family, though, the value also includes the life style opportunity for those who want to farm.

The question isn't whether or not the family and the farm should stay together. The question is how do we arrange things so that the farmers in the family have a farm to run, and the non-farmers end up with the kind of inheritance that's "fair" for them.

PILLAR #3: ASSURING LIQUIDITY AND SECURITY.

This problem, liquidity, is simple to understand, but often complex to solve. In essence, this is the issue: there must be a provision made, somehow, to provide enough cash to pay the taxes that are going to be due on the owner's estate.

Fortunately, these taxes are definable in advance, so the problem needn't be one of surprise. The problem, instead, is that the family farm is almost by nature an illiquid investment — it isn't a quick source of cash. That source has to be planned out in advance, the farther in advance the better.

Here is one of the estate planning areas in which the farm owner needs competent professional advice. Someone (most likely an accountant, a banker, or experts in insurance and/or valuation) has to put together realistic estimates of estate taxes and death costs — and that's only half the job.

Once cash needs are determined, Dad, with professional guidance, has to decide where and how that cash will be found when needed — a highly technical and complex question requiring a great deal of expertise.

But before we can move on to minimizing taxes, we have to give some long thought to how the plan will assure a stable and liquid source of income for the previous owners. This means a comfortable income for Dad and Mom, and, eventually a secure income for the survivor of the two, which is usually Mom.

It's the lack of this kind of provision in an otherwise sound plan that leads Dad, subconsciously, to shelve the plan. He knows he wants something more, but isn't sure what.

What he wants, for him and Mom, is security, and if security's not in the plan, the plan probably won't be signed.

PILLAR # 4: MINIMIZING TAXES.

Our tax laws are a confused and dangerous minefield. An amateur is foolish for trying to find his way through them alone. Still, that very complexity allows a lot of flexibility in the actual planning process — for an expert who knows the laws and the techniques.

There are many ways to minimize taxes, and professional tax experts spend their professional lives exploring these methods and even devising new approaches. But does the farm owner use them or take advantage of all the time they've spent pouring over the books? Nope. Instead, they try to answer the questions themselves. Or they ask about a "good book" on the subject. *"Somebody mentioned something about a '303 Redeemer.' Where can I find out about that?"*

There are a lot of ways to minimize the taxable value of the farm, or to set up gifting programs, or to transfer equity growth during the owner's life. But these are complex solutions and they require experts.

Still, the requirement for expert help doesn't relieve the farm owner of his basic responsibilities. He doesn't have to be a tax expert to plan his estate, but he does have to have wisdom and he does have to make the ultimate decisions. Nobody can sign the plan for him. His responsibility is to keep the big picture in mind at all times, to juggle all the conflicting goals, to see the differences and similarities among his heirs.

His job is to ensure that the farm and the family survive intact. If you think that requires the wisdom of Solomon, you're right, but the farm owner has an advantage over Solomon. All the important questions have been asked — and answered —

somewhere before by other family farmers.

Dad doesn't have to decide alone.

WHY OUTSIDE HELP IS ESSENTIAL

The above aren't the only questions facing a family farm in transition. There are always ongoing business and financial decisions to be made.

But the above succession and continuity issues are the most fundamental concerns of estate planning. They arise out of the natural course of events, out of the farm's passage through its life cycle, out of the dilution of ownership control, and out of the increasing differences among the heirs and owners.

The existence of these problems isn't a black mark against the owners. The problems are as natural as, say, rebellion in a teenager. The trick in either case is to survive the process intact so that the benefits of the resulting changes can be enjoyed.

Estate planning raises a lot of technical questions. Competent technical help will be required, to be sure. There are many financial, legal, tax, and organizational issues to be addressed. But even capable technical advisors will find it difficult to operate unless there is understanding and agreement among the owners. That often requires the help of outsiders, too.

Dad should assume there will almost always be some disagreement among his heirs, particularly if they are of the third, or following generations. This inevitability should be assumed, accepted, and worked with. Decisions about the future should be made with those differing goals and attitudes placed in the balance.

The farm owner's goal in planning — his primary goal, more important than tax savings or immediate "fairness" — should be encouraging and maintaining family agreement. And that agreement is best based on the mutual desire to do what's best for the farm.

Trouble is, we can all lose our way in this kind of agreement. Time and events, and even age tend to change our perspectives. After a while, some of what we believed, we no longer believe. Things change. And a good estate plan takes these inevitable changes into account.

Here is where competent, informed, and respected professional advisors really earn their fees. They have the objectivity and knowledge to see when things are going wrong, and they have the expertise to help put them right again.

All we have to do is learn to use them . . . and, ultimately, to trust them.

But farmers are universally suspicious, and, as a result, have not sought out the kind of expert advice necessary to do some of the more sophisticated forms of planning.

The Farm Bureau in Ohio did a survey in 1980 covering legal services. A great number of forms were mailed out to farmers who were asked questions like "How far would you drive to . . . get a will, get a divorce lawyer, etc." They covered everything from a simple will to a total restructure of the business and the estate plan.

Even though these different areas generally require different kinds of expertise which is usually unavailable locally, the response was three to one that farmers would go no further than the county seat to get help.

The ability to get help is a real stumbling block for farmers in the estate planning process. True, top-notch professional help is not always the easiest thing to find, and it is particularly difficult to find *specialists* in some of the more complex areas, but it's not impossible — nor is it the only problem.

The farmer has another fear, too, the fear of being taken advantage of, and this can be his most powerful reason for avoiding the advisors he needs.

Well, if the advice were not so important to his future, the future of his farm, and the future of his family, we suppose it would be okay for him to give in to his distrust. But the advice is critical to the most important areas of his life.

In some ways, the successful farmer is like the young girl who went out with a few real jerks on her first few dates. Under these circumstances, her desire to enter a convent would be perfectly understandable — but not necessarily in her best interest.

So, maybe it's understandable that the family farmer has the urge to contemplate the handling of his estate in his own personal monastery. But that doesn't mean it's in his own best interest, either.

Good advisors, like God-fearing, responsible young men, are out there in the world. They just take a little looking for.

And, surely, both are worth the search.

Chapter 13
BASIC ESTATE PLANNING TECHNIQUES —
WILLS AND TRUSTS

One thing is sure, when we get the shovel's final pat on the butt, we'll be taking nothing with us. We have to "give it all away" sometime, to someone.

The difference between us is that some plan it properly — making the tough judgments about when to give it, in what measure, and to whom — while others leave estate planning to the cold hand of the law (which should be called "estate plundering").

Many farm owners seem to fall in that second class. They spend most of their time building their operations. They concentrate on short-term survival, growth, and farming decisions (all worthwhile and necessary, of course) — and usually have very little time left for long-term planning.

This is understandable. Reaching success, particularly in agriculture today, is tough. But keeping that success in the long term is also tough, and getting tougher all the time. What's long-term planning? It's looking down the road five, 10 or 15 years for ways to protect the results of all the hard work of the current generations on the farm — and all the generations who have gone before us.

It may be understandable that we don't plan, but it isn't excusable. Failure to plan for continuation of the operation can be a fatal mistake.

DISASTER CAN HAPPEN TOMORROW

I've got time.

When any harassed and overworked farm owner is asked to look into the future, that's what he says. I'll get around to it. One of these days, we're going to have to look into that.

Sure. Like the growing season's going to get four months longer.

Well, according to the statistics, many of us just won't have the time. Recent studies indicate that the odds of dying or becoming disabled before retirement are very high. For example, a 45-year-old man has about a 25% chance of dying before he is 65. If that individual is in business with his brother there is a 44% chance that one of them will die before retirement. With three brothers working together, the chance is 58%. Sure, these are only statistics, but who wants to take the chance of proving them wrong?

Besides, in agriculture — not the world's safest occupation — the odds are even higher that one of the owners will become disabled before retirement.

What does all this imply? It means that without a sound estate plan, there is a very good chance that the farmers in the family will lose control of the farm.

Here, in easily predictable steps, is what probably will happen without such a workable estate plan:

1) *The attorneys will begin the legal proceedings.*

2) *The bankers will either restrict the credit or call in the loans.*

3) *The creditors will push harder to be paid.*

4) *The debtors will disappear.*

5) *Employees will get nervous* (and even though most farms don't have a lot of high-level non-family employees, even the less essential people can cause problems if they're unsure of their future).

6) *Family members will need cash.*

7) *The Government will want its tax payments.*

8) *Hospitals will become family meeting places.*

9) *Family income will begin to drop.*

Any one of these, by itself, could reduce the value or the efficiency of the operation, but together they can rip the bottom out of the net worth of any family farm. They can even threaten its very existence.

YOU'VE GOT TO KNOW YOUR TOOLS

In previous chapters, we've been encouraging the family farmer to make all the tough judgments early, up front, and for himself. But this thinking is still not enough. Making the personal judgments about ourselves and our heirs isn't the end. We still have to put those judgments into effect. And, for that, we need a good set of tools.

Estate planning tools are best used in the hands of specialists, but it's *our* estate, not theirs. The final decisions about which tools to use and which course to take still rest with the farm owner. This is why the successful farmer, like any other business owner, needs to understand the tools available to him, their features, and their limitations. This kind of knowledge will help his thinking, and help him make sense of what he needs to do.

This isn't a book on estate planning, but since planning is so critically important to the continuation of the family farm, we have devoted the next two chapters to an elementary discussion of the basic tools of the estate planning process.

But, remember, we said "elementary." What's here is not intended as a substitute for professional advice.[1] *(This isn't a boiler plate "disclaimer," by the way. We believe there is no substitute for professional advice.)*

First, we'll deal with the most common tools, wills and trusts. In the next chapter, we'll discuss the more complex issue of buy/sell agreements.

WHY "GET AROUND TO" WRITING A WILL?

Most of us have a lot of reasons for not writing wills, many of them very complicated. Human beings are pros at rationalizing inaction and excusing a lot of bad decisions, and the reasons for not writing a will lead the rationalization pack. But don't let the involved explanations fool you. Most of them boil down to one of these:

1) *"It's so complicated, I don't know where to begin."*

2) *"I can't decide what to do."*

3) *"I don't have the time."*

4) *"All of the above."*

Too complicated? Well, it's true that estate planning isn't an amateur's sport, but that's why professional advisors exist. It's not too complicated for them. It's their specialty. This excuse is really a smoke screen for the failure to find and use the best advisors available.

Can't decide? Well, that's what much of the preceding chapters was about. And, once again, when professional advisors become involved, the options can become clearer and choices are naturally easier.

No time? This one is true, but in the opposite sense it's usually meant. Whatever time each of us has left, it's never going to be enough to do everything we want to do. And if the Great Accountant decides to close our books early, we have even less time. There is no time. No time to wait.

If you're still skeptical, let's look at the consequences of doing nothing. Actually, it's hard to "do nothing." Not having a will is, in itself, a form of estate planning. It's a decision to let the *state* deal with our property rather than doing it ourselves.

State governments aren't nice people, nor are they our neighbors. They're bureaucracies, and they're run with the interests of "all the people" in mind, which rarely is the same as the interests of any one person or family. It's unlikely, at best, that governments will do things the way we would do them. They're more likely, in fact, to do just the opposite.

WITHOUT A WILL, *all of our legal heirs will be treated equally,* even if they have different needs or we wanted to treat them differently. For example, say there are certain heirs who have significant support needs (e.g. children with special medical or educational needs), while others are in very comfortable financial circumstances. Sure, we could expect our heirs to take care of each other, but why should we force the decision on them?

WITHOUT A WILL, *it's impossible to designate who is going to get specific items*, such as Grandma's rocking chair or Granddad's old watch. It doesn't matter whether Dad wanted Timmy to have the watch or not. If he dies intestate, possession of that watch will be settled by free-for-all. It's human nature. The most insignificant of items can become suddenly priceless if somebody else is going to get them.

The chance of getting personal effects of a deceased relative, as we all know, is governed by the law of increasing distance. The farther away you are when the folks die, the less likely it is you'll end up with the things Mom "promised" you. One elderly lady we know recently had the uplifting experience of buying back at auction the bed she slept in as a teenager. Her brother had "said" it was hers, but didn't get around to a will.

This kind of experience can be terribly divisive in families, particularly farm families, where relationships are so important. We all know people who haven't spoken for 20 years because, say, the quilt their great-grandmother wanted them to have *"ended up in the house of That Woman, who wasn't even part of the family until she married in."*

WITHOUT A WILL, *you can't choose your estate representative,* the person who's going to be responsible for settling your estate. Most of us (and particularly farmers who want to maintain privacy) would much rather have a member of the family do this than some stranger chosen by a court. Further, if the court demands that this stranger post a bond to protect the estate, another expense is incurred. Assuming the person we choose for this role in our will is trusted, this requirement, and expense, can be waived in writing.

WITHOUT A WILL, *a farm operating as a proprietorship or partnership, will be closed down until the estate is settled.* Given the seasonal nature of agriculture, it's usually vital that business be continued without interruption. Trouble is, operating without authorization (through a will), a representative is exposed to all sorts of liability. The sensible thing for him or her to do would be to halt operations and eliminate the liability. A properly devised will, on the other hand, could authorize the estate representative to continue the business without fear of being held liable.

WITHOUT A WILL, *it's impossible to choose the guardians for minor* or handicapped children. Courts will do their best, but the person they choose is not likely to be the person Mom or Dad would've chosen if they had the chance — or, more accurately, if they'd used the chance they had.

WITHOUT A WILL, *there's no way to protect incompetent or unprepared heirs from their own foolishness or lack of ability,* something easily done through trusts set up in a will.

WITHOUT A WILL, *it's often very difficult to take advantage of the large number of approved tax-saving estate planning techniques,* most important of which, as hinted above, is the trust. Trusts are described below.

There are other problems, but these should be enough to encourage any thinking person to reexamine the excuses for not having a will.

The next question, then, is "what is a will?"

WILLS

In essence, a will is a legal declaration of what someone wants done with his or her possessions after death. Simple enough. It's simply a vehicle by which intentions are made known.

With the proper professional help in writing the will, most of us don't need to know much more than this. But we do need to think through what we want our will to accomplish, so our legal advisors can write it properly. Failure to *think* about what we're doing too often results in inadequate guidance for the advisor and, thereafter, an inadequate will — better than nothing, but not by much.

The most common inadequate will is the so-called "I Love You Will." This is a will that says (in 50,000 words) something like:

> "*. . . everything to Mom when Dad dies, then divided equally among the kids after she's gone.*"

The "I Love You Will," generally useless though it is, does accomplish one purpose very well. It expresses how the person who wrote the will feels (or felt) about his heirs. Unfortunately, it usually fails at the most important purpose: delivering what the deceased intended, or what the heirs want and need. A will should be much more than an expression of emotion.

Just consider the major problems that can arise out of the "I Love You Will:"

1) **TAX EXPENSE.** Giving it all to Mom, where the estate is big enough to be subject to taxation, fails to take advantage of potential estate tax savings.

2) **BURDEN ON THE HEIRS.** The subsequent equal division among the kids places a

tremendous burden on the farm heirs.

The on-farm heirs are burdened with the responsibility of buying out their brothers and sisters, typically at a "fair market" price. Then they have to pay their proportionate share of the taxes on the estate. Since this is impossible for an estate that has no cash but lots of assets, assets will have to be sold.

But the sale of assets sells the ability to earn money to pay back the cash that was borrowed to pay the taxes — a vicious circle and one that's often terminal.

Typical "I Love You Wills" cause more problems than most people can imagine. This isn't because they're simple, however. Good, effective wills don't have to be complex. In fact, a will that's simple, but that clearly states what is to happen to the assets, can be a very effective and inexpensive tool — one that, today, can accomplish much more than ever before.

Every will must address the "4 Pillars" we talked about in Chapter 12, in order to effectively achieve its basic purpose: providing the simple, but powerful first step in planning for passing down the farm.

TRUSTS

We could literally write thousands of pages describing trusts as they apply to estate planning. But this isn't a how-to book. It's a "why?" book. So rather than a lot of intricate detail about the makeup of trusts from a lawyer's perspective, we'll just explore the basic concepts and explain the benefits of using trusts in passing down the farm to future generations.

The first and most natural question, of course, is why does someone need a trust if they have a will? The explanation is tied to the difference between wanting something to happen and finding ways to make it happen. Primarily, a will is only a declaration of *intent*. A trust is a vehicle for making sure that declaration is *carried out*.

As we could gather from it's name, a trust is a tool used to "trust" somebody else (the "trustee") to administer assets for our heirs (the "beneficiaries"). Since our heirs could do whatever they want with estate assets once they owned them outright, a trust is a way to limit their options.

By designing a trust, the farm owner (the "donor") separates ownership of the assets (which belongs to the trust) from the right to benefit from them (which belongs to the beneficiaries). This way, he can, in many cases, help ensure a wise and beneficial use of the assets.

Another way to look at a trust is as an artificial person, which can either be born during the life of the creator or at the creator's death. Either way, its mission in life is to act on behalf of someone — and for the benefit of them or their heirs.

Sounds complicated already, right? Why would someone even bother to get into designing a trust?

Because there are a lot of potential benefits.

BENEFITS OF TRUSTS

One principal benefit is *tax savings*. When a trust is activated , the donor generally gives up title to the assets or property to someone else. Trusts can be set up during your lifetime (inter vivos), with the assets remaining in your name until death (activation). There is no requirement to give things away to a trust to set it up. If done correctly, a trust is a means for removing assets from the donor's taxable estate, potentially saving estate taxes and other costs. Also, any income from the assets or property will thereafter be taxed in a separate, possibly lower, tax bracket.

But, as we've said before, we don't believe tax savings are the most important goal of estate planning. Nor are they the most important goal of trust design. The fact is, trusts can have a number of non-tax advantages that can be very important, indeed.

The principal advantage is the transfer of title to, and responsibility for management of, property to people who are capable managers, whether or not they are beneficiaries.

Given that farm owners often worry their heirs won't be able to handle their inheritance — because of lack of experience, incompetence, potential disagreement, irresponsibility, etc. — a trust could provide a number of needed advantages:

1) **The Protection of the Law.** Trusts have been the law for centuries. The legal precedents around them are among the strongest and the most strictly adhered to. A trust, in fact, is one of the strongest protections that can be put around one's intentions for property.

2) **Control.** Trusts can be written in very detailed ways. This gives the donor great flexibility in stating just what can and cannot be done with the property or assets in the trust. We can, for example, designate the age at which people can receive property — a great advantage if we believe 18 or 21-year-olds are too young. In effect, this is the power to control and protect assets even after death. (Maybe, in some ways, we can take it with us?)

3) **Protection of Beneficiaries.** There are many cases where a farm owner's beneficiaries are inexperienced, uninterested, or maybe even incompetent to handle the burdens of managing property and assets. Yet the owner's desire may be to have these heirs benefit somehow from what he's built. A trust can be designed to place responsibility for managing and protecting the assets in the hands of someone more capable of handling the responsibility — a relative who's an experienced farmer, for example.

This is especially important in situations where Mom's security could wind up dependent on the skills of inexperienced heirs. A trust, empowered along with Mom, can hire professional farm management until the heirs are ready.

4) **Competent Management.** With a trust, a farm owner can separate asset benefit from asset management. This assures protection for all his heirs, while increasing the chances the assets will be well managed.

THE DISTRUST OF TRUSTS

Despite all these advantages, however, trusts are not all that common down on the farm.

Most family farmers don't really understand what a trust is, and even assume *"trusts are for rich people, not us poor farmers."* Besides, many farmers think, trusts always require "trustees," right? And that is an awful thought to Dad.

He, like many of today's successful farmers, remembers those Depression-era movies. He saw Shirley Temple being taken advantage of by some banker. It's an old theme — the little girl or the helpless widow, locked in the attic, while the evil guardian or trustee takes all of the money.

"We've worked too hard," the farmer says, *"to turn it over to someone we don't know, and who doesn't know farming."*

If the idea of a trustee isn't fearful enough, consider who encourages Dad to set up these trusts (the farm owner's advisors, whom he doesn't particularly trust), and who promotes them (the banks — and everybody knows how he feels about banks).

Dad can't shake this picture of the widow's lawyer/trustee winding up with all the money (while the bank, of course, gets the farm).

Dad's got a lot of these negative pictures he can drag out of the closet. We all remember (or have heard of) the first bank holiday. Well, look, Dad says, why make the bank the trustee of Mom's income? That bank could disappear. We're not going to let that happen to us.

Right. We shouldn't let it happen, and it doesn't have to. Such "evils" can be avoided while we take full advantage of the flexibility of trusts. The fact is, tools like living trusts, marital deduction trusts, and others are *very* effective means for accomplishing management and tax planning objectives of both the senior generation and the heirs.

And they can be set up without putting control in the hands of strangers.

For example, one of the more competent sons can be a co-trustee along with Mom. The bank need only be there as an advisor. Other arrangements are possible, too, but the point is that the family can be kept in control. After all, bankers don't understand much about running a farm, so why should anybody leave them in total charge of one?

Remember, estate planning is more than just dying neatly. It's being able to live with the plans you've put together for the benefit of others.

TYPES OF TRUSTS

Trusts can be described according to whether they're activated after the donor's death and the will is probated (called "testamentary" trusts), or during the donor's life ("living" trusts). The distinction is important.

In recent years, living trusts have grown increasingly popular for a number of good reasons. They're not always the answer, but in many situations they can do just as much as testamentary trusts, sometimes more.

Their primary advantage is that they can be made either *revocable* or *irrevocable*. A revocable trust, of course, is one that the donor can change or call off any time he wishes. This provides wonderful flexibility for a farm owner who wants to try out what he thinks is a good plan and a good trustee before committing to it.

A living trust can be *"funded."* For example, the farm could be sold and the proceeds placed in a living trust, perhaps managed by a corporate trustee, who would invest the funds for the creator and subsequently for his spouse and heirs.

On the other hand, the trust could be *"unfunded."* These are typically set up in so-called "pour-over wills." Specific assets are directed to specific individuals (Grandma's quilt to Susie and Dad's shotgun to Junior) with the balance of the estate assets being "poured over" into the trust where it is managed for the beneficiaries.

Often in conjunction with an unfunded living trust, you will find a life insurance policy. This policy might be owned by and payable to the trust at the death of the trust's creator. This technique allows life insurance proceeds to flow into the hands of the beneficiaries in a tax-efficient way, while at the same time, providing professional management of this sum of money.

The living trust can also avoid some estate settlement costs, since the trust property won't transfer under the will. Further, this avoids both the delays and publicity of probate.

There's a price paid for flexibility, however. The tax laws don't give *revocable* trusts any estate tax breaks, since the donor never really gives up the property. Still, the tradeoff is usually worth it. Revocable living trusts are usually set up by worried farm owners, who feel very uncomfortable setting up something irrevocable without testing the assumptions involved. As one farmer put it: *"There's no sense taking off your clothes until you're ready for bed."*

Whatever kind of living trust is involved, however, the idea is very simple. In a typical situation, the will (pour-over) conveys to the trustee what is left of the estate after the debts have been paid and the various specific bequests have been made.

These assets, then, are added to those that are already in the trust, if any, and then they are administered according to the terms of the trust, as part of the assets of the trust.

An important note to repeat here is that *the trustee is just that — someone you can trust.* And it's your choice. The trustee could be your banker, or lawyer, or it could be one of the kids. It could also be all or some of the kids working together with the advice of the lawyer and the banker. Any combination of people and institutions is generally acceptable.

The key is to make sure that the people who are the trustees can be trusted (not from a legal sense, necessarily, but trusted to carry out your wishes fully). Then you want to make sure that those wishes most important to you get the highest priority in the mind of the trustee.

For example, say that saving the farm from being sold to pay taxes is your most important goal. If for some reason that's not possible, you want your second most important goal — taking care of your spouse — to be accomplished before the balance of the assets are divided up among the children, the local charities, and so forth.

These priorities should be clearly spelled out in the trust, and a trustee chosen who you feel will want, and be able, to protect those priorities.

SOME NECESSARY DETAILS

If you understand nothing else about trusts, get at least this clearly in mind:

A trust is a highly refinable, very flexible and extremely useful means by which a farmer, property owner, whoever, may separate the burden of property ownership from the benefits of property ownership.

Because of its inherent flexibility, a trust allows the farm owner to do all this:

- *to whatever degree, and*

- *on whatever terms, and*

- *for whatever period of time (within the limits imposed by law), and*

- *for the benefit of whomever he wishes.*

That's a powerful tool, whatever way you look at it. Of course, the trustee charges a fee for the services, but that fee is an investment in the future of our own wishes.

A few remaining items:

THE "JOINT TRUSTEE." The amount of responsibility given to the trustee is almost always completely within the control of the person who creates the trust. This is important because the situation could exist whereby the trustee (Junior, for example) may be an excellent farmer, but doesn't know anything about investing money. In this case, a joint trustee relationship can be created which would give the banker charge of the investing and junior charge of the farm operation.

This ability to shift among several people the levels of responsibility and accountability gives the trust's creator the ability to get the best possible management of the assets.

BENEFICIAL INTEREST. Few farm families have clear-cut situations such as the only heir of an only heir. More likely, there are a number of heirs, maybe some cousins from a partnership, along with a combination of on-farm and off-farm heirs.

> *"My sons want the farm,"* the farm owner could be wondering, *"but what about my daughter in town? How do I take care of her?"*

Here the creator of the trust is able to determine just how much each beneficiary can benefit and in what way. Take the above concern, for example. The farm owner could, in his trust, earmark certain non-farm assets such as life insurance proceeds, cash, investments, etc. to be available for the off-farm daughter in town. If, however, he were fortunate enough to have a long life and the assets multiplied tremendously, he may eventually change the trust to indicate that any estate taxes should be paid by the liquid assets, with the balance going to the daughter, leaving the farm intact for the on-farm heirs.

As another option, and depending on the mix of assets available, he could leave liquid assets and farm assets to off-farm and on-farm heirs respectively, with additional provisions, if necessary, for a buy-out of the off-farm heirs by those who stayed on the farm.

Trusts are extremely flexible, and can allow for special

divisions. Maybe there's a hunting lodge in Michigan in the estate. It may not have the value of the farm, but it might be just the thing an off-farm heir would want because that's where he and Dad always went hunting. This kind of provision may be more important than an absolutely equal division of assets.

Beneficial interests can also be *"successive,"* in that after one generation is through with the assets, the trust can continue on for another generation or two, so long as it is within the law.

In this way, Dad can either provide a blueprint that is a tax-wise method of passing down the estate assets, or he can provide handcuffs that direct how succeeding generations handle his property.

The potential flexibility is enormous, but, unfortunately, most farm owners don't use this tool at all. They tend to stick to very simple types of living trusts. Why? Two reasons. First of all, farm owners feel somehow like dictators setting up complicated blueprints for their heirs down the generations. Secondly, the farmer's advisors often aren't specialized enough to be able to propose multi-generational plans.

It's not our intention to say beneficial interest trusts are necessarily good or bad. It's enough that we point out the fact that they exist as options, and they require experts to design them *according to the goals defined by the farm owner.*

INSURANCE TRUSTS. Because farm businesses are generally asset-rich and cash-poor, insurance trusts have been used by sophisticated advisors for the last several years to create cash at death for the payment of transfer costs, taxes, and even in some cases to provide funds for the non-farm heirs' inheritances.

The simplest description of an insurance trust is any trust whose main job is to receive and then to manage the insurance proceeds, for the benefit of a beneficiary or group of beneficiaries. Here, we have an opportunity to create the answer to liquidity needs at death in a tax-wise way, and to do so on the installment plan through the purchase of a life insurance policy.

Our experience has been that these trusts are seldom used

by farm owners. First of all, most farmers don't have enough life insurance to make such a trust worthwhile. On top of this, the working relationship most farmers have with their advisors isn't good enough to even allow the topic to come up in conversation. This is unfortunate, because they are often missing out on important planning opportunities.

FARMERS, ADVISORS, AND INSURANCE AGENTS

Consider the typical farm owner's relationship with his advisors.

First, there is his lawyer, assuming he has one. In many cases, farm owners have a series of lawyers they've used for various jobs over the years, but there's no consistent relationship with any one of them. But if he does have a relationship with a single attorney, it's generally for the wrong reasons. He's Dad's lawyer because, well, he always has been, or he's a deacon at the church, or he went to high school with Mom. He may be competent, too, but that's seldom the primary criterion.

Then there's his insurance agent. The little insurance the farmer does have was most likely bought from a succession of individual agents who managed to catch him with good digestion or a specific worry.

He buys insurance as a band aid or because he vaguely thinks he "should." Since he's not too chummy with insurance people, though, the farm owner encourages these individual agents to move on, permanently. As a result, no insurance agent is close enough to him, over enough time, to get into the subject of an insurance trust.

This leaves it as something Dad has to bring up with his lawyer and accountant, which (because he's not so excited about them, either) he never gets around to doing. This is why we find so many farm owners with chains of insurance policies. The amount of coverage generally has nothing to do with the size of the need, only with the ability of specific (and long gone) agents to extract premium dollars.

It's common for us to find a dozen different insurance policies, none of which are payable to a trust. Most of them are owned by the wrong people, designed to work with laws that have been off the books for years.

One farmer, 63, with whom we worked on succession planning, had purchased a policy with the face amount of $10,000 about 18 months before we met him. He paid the premium for one year, then failed to renew the policy. When we asked why he didn't renew it, he said he didn't know why he bought it and didn't know what good it would do. His needs, in fact, so far outstripped the features of that policy, that it had no meaning for him.

Later, after knowledgeable professionals were brought together and the estate, business and succession planning were done, insurance of $250,000 was purchased. That policy remained in place until the farmer died. He kept the new policy in force, despite the expense, because he could see exactly how it fit into his plans and how his premium dollars were buying benefit for the family.

While still on the subject of advisors, we want to emphasize how important it is to separate the generalists from the specialists. The advisors most readily available to the successful farmer are more likely to be generalists. Because of their location and the ongoing needs of their clients, they have to know something about everything. This is proper and appropriate for helping clients day to day.

But the farmer makes life difficult for his "generalist," since he hardly uses him at all. When he does, it's usually with thinly disguised grumbling about how much he costs. This makes for a very shaky relationship, and if the generalist comes across a problem that requires a specialist, he hesitates. *"If I refer him to a specialist, he'll probably decide I don't know anything — or, worse, he'll think that the specialist has the same kind of wide knowledge I do. Either way, I'll lose him as a client and he won't be getting any advice at all."*

These fears aren't unfounded. Advisors have lost clients this way, and would hate to make that mistake again. What's needed is an open, trusting, and realistic relationship between the farm owner and his advisors. The farmer needs the generalist, both because he can provide the best understanding of the overall situation and also for reliable referrals to competent specialists. The generalist advisor needs the specialist to help him and his client through the knottier problems. All the farm owner and his advisor need is to understand each other's position. That way a lot of bad advice and dragging of heels can be avoided.

And maybe some estate planning could even get done.

In summary, wills and trusts make up what we call the "simple" solutions, simple in the sense that they're not all that involved and they should be done now. Without them, you're cruising for long-term disaster. They also have short-term benefits, in that they can solve today's problems *and* tomorrow's.

Tomorrow's problems often require something more, as well. People change. Families change. Farm operations grow and diversify. Each of these changes, and others, will have an effect on the additional estate planning tools needed.

The farm operation, for example, can outstrip the plan. Wills and trusts are only beneficial for the first $1.5 million or so of estate value. What happens if the value of the farm jumps to $10 million?

What happens if one partner wants to retire? What about disagreements with the IRS over value? How can multiple families work the same farm without being distracted by "who's getting more than whom?"

The answers to these and related questions are usually found in more sophisticated approaches to estate planning, beginning with basic buy/sell agreements, the subject of the next chapter.

Stick with us on the technical stuff. It's worth it.

---

[1]*(It isn't our intent to practice law. Any advice as to the use of a trust and how it should be drawn up should come from your attorney. The purpose of this very general discussion is to get you to the point where you feel comfortable discussing these tools with your advisors.)*

CHAPTER 14
BASIC ESTATE PLANNING TECHNIQUES —
BUY/SELL AGREEMENTS

Wills and trusts, valuable and necessary as they are, usually fall short of solving some of the most important transition problems the successful family farm faces — particularly the problems that occur if, God forbid, the owners stay living!

But the unexpected (and, of course, desired) long life of the owners isn't the only possible problem.

- *What about the heirs?*

- *What if some want to farm, then change their minds?*

- *What about partners?*

- *What about retirement of one or more owners?*

- *Or, even more likely, what about the disability of the owner?*

Wills and trusts, effective and necessary as they are, can't do much to answer these questions.

We're dealing, here, with questions of *transferring the ownership of a farm operation among the living* — within the family or outside — to solve the problems of the living.

EXAMPLES WHERE BUY/SELL AGREEMENTS APPLY

Consider some typical situations:

● *Two brothers own a successful operation. One has two young daughters. The other has three grown sons who want to farm. One of the brothers wants to retire.*

Wouldn't each of the brother/partners want a "fair" outcome for their children? But how can the three on-farm sons be expected to treat their young female cousins fairly? And what is "fair," after all?

● *Three heirs inherit the farm, but two know they will eventually want to sell to the one who runs the operation.*

How do the three siblings handle the fact that only one of them runs the operation, while the two off-farm together hold control of the business? Wouldn't it be better if they had some previously accepted guidelines for solving their problems?

● *A father, son, and uncle are working a farm successfully, until one day an accident disables the uncle. He can't work, but needs income.*

What happens to the disabled uncle who spent his life building a farm operation that, suddenly, when he's disabled, can't (or won't) buy out his share at a "fair" price? Shouldn't he be able to come away whole — and shouldn't his brother and nephew be able to protect the operation from a sudden bloodletting of cash?

> • *Two partners each wonder what the other partner will do with his share if he wants to sell? What if we stop getting along, they wonder, (after all, our wives are already at odds)? How can we each be sure the other won't tie up the whole thing by demanding a ridiculous amount for his share?*

Aren't they right to worry that their good working relationship might someday be destroyed? And shouldn't they be able to solve their problem before that happens? Wouldn't one or the other want to take over the business if the other couldn't or wouldn't continue? Wouldn't both want full value for his interest if he left, but at the same time want first option on the operation if the other chooses to leave?

These are only a sample of the kinds of concerns that come up. Wills and trusts can do little if anything to solve these problems.

There are answers, though. Basically, each owner can agree to sell his interest to the other at a set price if he dies, retires, or otherwise leaves the operation. Or the business itself can agree to purchase the parting owner's interest. These are simple arrangements, easy to understand, which can be essential to the continuity of the farm.

The key points are to develop agreement, up front, *before it's needed*, then plan ways to come up with the necessary cash.

OPTIONS FOR MOVING ASSETS

In case you still wonder why this is important, just consider the options available to a farm family that needs to move assets to solve some particular problem. Basically, there are three:

1) **LIQUIDATE.** This involves selling off the assets one at a time. However, in liquidation

good farm land may bring a reasonable price, but the depreciated equipment might sell for 10 cents on the dollar.

A friend of ours, an auctioneer, describes an auction as a process that turns dollars into pennies. Everyone who goes to an auction goes to get a bargain. Hardly anyone goes to help out his neighbor.

2) **SELL ENTIRELY TO A THIRD PARTY.** Historically, this hasn't been very successful in the farm world, but, due to the present shakeup in agriculture, we believe there will be more and more situations where farmers will sell their entire business. Properly planned, this can be an effective approach, but it's still the exception rather than the rule.

3) **PASS IT ON WITHIN THE FAMILY.** Letting surviving spouses, children or other family members run the operation is the most common goal of the family farmer. All that's necessary, if one or another owner wants/needs to get out, is some affordable way to do so.

But . . .

. . . *But* agriculture is big business. Whether the family wants to stay in the business themselves or a partner does, or whether the heirs want to take it over, or whether it's simply going to be sold outside, these sales have to be carefully put together.

For example, if a farm owner decides to sell to an outsider, or even to his brother, he may have trouble making sure that his family gets the maximum value for his interest.

WHY BUYERS OFFER LESS THAN IT'S "WORTH"

Potential buyers, whether they are family or not, will offer less than the operation's real worth for at least two reasons:

1) *The owner's efforts and knowledge probably contributed a lot to the profits that the farm has earned. Margins in agriculture are so slim that the skills of the operator often provide the margin of victory. If he or she is no longer around, profits can disappear and the operation's earning power will be greatly reduced.*

We usually expect mistakes to be made after a farm changes owners in any manner. These mistakes are the kind the previous owner wouldn't have made (or made, and learned from, long ago, when the cost of making them was much less).

There are two levels of business mistakes. One the business absorbs, the other absorbs the business. The risk of the latter reduces the value of the operation to a potential buyer.

Also, marketing in agriculture has become more and more important as the profit center. If the previous owner's knowledge produces the profits, buyers won't be willing to pay top dollar for underlying assets if that knowledge isn't part of the package.

2) *The purchase price will be arrived at through negotiation.* This is a major difficulty faced by family and non-family alike. Potential buyers will offer less than the asking price, and the final price will be the result of a compromise reflecting the bargaining strength of the two parties.

For example, if Brother A runs the operation and the widow of Brother B is to get a passive income, who has the bargaining power? Who's in the stronger position once Brother B is gone?

In general, potential buyers will have more leverage and more control over the price than the sellers. In these situations, the seller or the seller's heirs are likely to get less than full value for what the seller built.

One farm we know, operated by two brothers, faces a problem like this. One owner, 55, had three boys, all of whom now say they want to be on the farm. One is 23 and very much involved. The other two sons are still in tech school. The other brother married late in life and had two little girls, each under 10 years old. When the second brother died of a heart attack, his wife (who didn't have a farm background) was left in a tough position. She had to take what was available to her.

In this case, there was an agreement, but it was based on a valuation of the business which, at the time of the brother's death, happened to be depressed. The widow wound up with some life insurance proceeds and a promise of some income over the next 10 years.

In sum, the situation is a mess. The surviving brother, who's trying to bring his three boys into the business has lost his partner and has nobody to replace him. His sons aren't ready for real responsibility, and the widow isn't a farmer. Worse, if they pay any income from their farm corporation to the widow, other than what small amount was stipulated by the agreement, it will be considered a dividend by the IRS (since she has no farm experience and can't work there). That extra money would then be both taxable to her and non-deductible to the corporation. This is really the worst of all worlds for them.

What makes this situation ironic is the fact that their insurance agent had approached them a few years before with a program for fully insuring the buy out agreement. This plan would've liquidated the widow's interest fairly, with no huge cash outlay from the corporation.

They were going to "think about it," and did so until the now deceased brother had his first heart attack and became uninsurable. At that point, the insurance option was closed, and they knew they didn't have a lot of time to do something else. Worse, they also knew the corporation couldn't generate enough cash to lay something aside for the widow.

What they have now is a very difficult time for everybody. The surviving brother and his son are working hard to meet the provisions of the agreement, yet they face the problem of barely affording the comforts they earn year to year, while the widow down the street is receiving only a fraction of the income she'd have if her husband were alive.

There is a way, however, to make sure stories like this

don't keep happening. The time to negotiate, settle, and fund sound agreements is *now*, while the parties to the agreement are in the best bargaining position. Looking ahead, a farm owner can fund his agreement with insurance, or seek out the potential buyers — whether they be neighbors, relatives, or some young person from the university — and negotiate an agreement with them which will give his family the most possible dollars for his hard work.

And the best (really the only) way to accomplish this is through a written contract, developed early and with care, which will establish the terms of the sale.

THE BUY/SELL AGREEMENT

A contract like this is referred to as a *buy/sell agreement*. It formalizes the way a farm will be turned over to new owners. It can provide for a smooth transition of ownership and minimize lost value for the family.

A buy/sell agreement is a mutual purchase/repurchase/ sale agreement between brothers, fathers and sons, siblings, cousins, fathers, sons and uncles — whoever. It's an agreement that can be drafted and updated frequently to reflect changing conditions. It's an agreement that lays out the terms and conditions under which the farm will change hands.

For example:

> • *If a cousin or a brother wants out, here is the formula for valuation, and this is how we're going to buy him out.*

> • *If grandfather dies, here's how we're going to buy grandmother out.*

> • *If uncle gets disabled, here is how we will assure that he has income continuation.*

A buy/sell is a combination sale, divorce and death agreement, negotiated up front in such a way that everybody is happy or just a bit unhappy (measures of sound negotiation). It should also contain a formula for future automatic updates.

Developing a legal and binding buy/sell is usually a very personal issue. It defines a legal relationship among *people*.

WHY USE A BUY/SELL?

This isn't to say that a buy/sell agreement is necessary for *every* business or estate plan. In simple situations — couples with no heirs, single children of single children, or even a case of two brothers who will inherit after Mom dies — a buy/sell would most likely be unnecessary (except the last example where the brothers would eventually need one between them).

The buy/sell becomes important in situations where there are owners (or potential owners) who may not have a *continuing* interest in the farm, for whatever reason. In such cases, buy/sell agreements offer three major advantages:

> 1) **They guarantee a market for an owner's interest at a fair price.** With a buy/sell agreement, an owner can be sure that his family will get a fair value for all of his hard work. It also guarantees that the family can avoid that disastrous "damage control," the post-death estate planning that tends to diminish the value of a business.
>
> 2) **They enable the remaining owners to retain control.** With a buy/sell agreement, an owner doesn't have to worry whether his partner's family will take over his partner's interest, or how they will be paid if they don't. He will know that he'll be in control of the business, that he'll be making the decisions, and that he can keep strangers out. Few farmers, for example, relish the thought of being in business with their sister-in-law.
>
> 3) **They can help avoid disputes with the IRS over estate taxes and estate valuation after an owner's death.** The IRS has its

own peculiar way of valuing a farm operation, which usually comes out higher than the value the executor uses on the estate tax return.

Let's look a little closer at Number 3, the buy/sell's value in future dealings with the Internal Revenue people.

BUY/SELLS AND THE IRS

The buy/sell keeps the IRS at bay because it states, in writing, that the business is worth so many dollars. The buy/sell is an agreement to sell for an amount today and tomorrow, and that agreement stops the IRS from successfully inflating the value.

Your executor and the IRS, of course, will have conflicting goals. Your executor wants to keep the value low to reduce your estate taxes. The IRS, on the other hand, wants a high value which will create more taxes. They rarely agree. Often, these disputes are decided in court, and there is a risk that the court will adopt the IRS's value rather than the executor's. If it does, your estate taxes will naturally increase as a result.

Of course, even if the court adopts your executor's value, there is usually a significant time delay before the case is decided. We have seen situations where two, three or four years pass before all this litigation ends. During that time your farm business is tied up, and your estate will have to pay some expensive legal bills.

A buy/sell agreement solves this problem by establishing a value for the farm and business which is binding on the IRS for estate tax purposes. If the agreement defines a price for which you are obligated to sell both during your life and at death, the IRS will not be able to value the business at a higher figure.

The agreement will also eliminate the delays and expenses which come with a court dispute.

FUNDING A BUY/SELL AGREEMENT

The buy/sell agreement alone, of course, is not enough unless it is backed by the funds to make it happen. If there's no money, the agreement is simply a worthless piece of paper. As a matter of fact, an unfunded buy/sell could force the family into actions it can't afford, creating more problems than it solves.

Funding for a buy/sell has to be planned in advance. There are four ways it can be done:

1) **Make regular contributions to an account earmarked for buying the business — a "Sinking Fund."** This is the "Christmas Club" approach to funding a buy/sell. It attempts to force the discipline of salting money away regularly. But, while a Christmas Club has the advantage of knowing when Christmas is coming, the buy/sell sinking fund doesn't allow for the unexpected death or disability of one of the parties to the agreement.

It takes a long time to put this sort of money aside, and there's no way of ensuring that time will be available.

2) **Borrow the money.** This sounds good, but it'll only work if a lender can be found who considers you and your business to be good credit risks. Given the fuzzy nature of agricultural lending these days, along with wide swings in interest rates, this isn't likely to be a secure funding approach for some time to come.

Borrowing should be the last resort, anyway, because it is the most expensive way to buy the business. The survivors will have to pay back what they borrowed, plus the interest on top of that. Look at some numbers:

Repaying a $500,000 loan over 10 years at 12% interest will cost $330,000 in interest alone. That, plus the $500,000 principal is $830,000. Think for a moment about what kind of gross sales will be necessary to come up with $830,000!

3) **Installment payments.** This seems like another way to fund the buy/sell, but it's not a lot different from borrowing the money. Here the heirs assume all the risk. The major difference between an installment sale and a loan from the bank is who has to wait to get their money.

For example, if a son is buying out the interest of his sisters, they will probably have to wait for 10, 15, or 20 years to receive the value of their inheritance. He, of course, has the use of it (the farm) from the beginning.

While it's true that most of the farms that were transferred in the previous generation were either passed through inheritance or an installment plan, income taxes and interest rates, as well as the present-day land values, make this as difficult as borrowing money from a bank.

4) **Life insurance.** In spite of the fact that few farmers "like" insurance, it happens often to be the most efficient way to fund a buy/sell agreement. With insurance, it's possible to know right away that the funds will be available exactly when they're needed.

There are also some hidden advantages with insurance ("hidden" because nobody but an insurance agent seems to understand them):

For one thing, when buying whole life insurance, one usually doesn't pay 100 cents on the dollar. With borrowing one always does. Also, life insurance is typically a budgetable expense at a time when both the insured and the business are healthy. Further, under present law, life insurance proceeds are income tax free and may be arranged to be estate tax free as well.

Here is one of the many situations in which professional advisors become critically important. The accountant, lawyer, and insurance representative should be used together to determine not only the basis of the buy/sell agreement, but also how it can best be funded.

By having all three of these people involved in the discussion, the farm owner is much more likely to wind up with an agreement that best fits the family's goals and objectives as well as the financial realities.

One caution: every advisor approaches planning from a unique point of view. While each viewpoint can be valid, no one of them is usually 100% on target from the farmer's point of view. The reason for bringing them together is to get the widest input. But that team needs an objective quarterback — either the farmer or a consultant calling the shots on his behalf.

IT DOESN'T HAVE TO BE COMPLEX

The majority of readers will probably find that updated wills with one or more trusts can effectively solve all or most of their estate tax problems. In many other cases, though, a buy/sell will fit in as the third, stabilizing leg.

These tools are reasonably simple and cost-efficient ways to deal with the estate and business planning process. Wills, trusts and buy/sell agreements can often be put together to get a secure and relatively inexpensive plan that does the job, without changing the way a person is doing business or living. And this, along with proper funding, can be done without any significant complications for the heirs.

There are cases, of course, where a buy/sell won't be enough. This is primarily a function of complexity — of the business, the family, and the goals — and the size of the business. At a certain point, an operation can become so large and complex that even a funded buy/sell agreement won't be able to do the job. Instead, the plan will have to shift the growth in the farm business to the operating heirs and/or make gifts of nonvoting interests to non-farm heirs.

With a really large operation, where, say, a son wants to buy out his two sisters, he has a major league problem. If he has to do that PLUS pay at least his third of the estate taxes, his situation just might be impossible.

In circumstances like this, where wills, trusts, and buy/sell agreements can't do the job, it's time to get into the more sophisticated areas of planning:

> 1) **Estate "Freezing."** These are techniques for passing future growth to the next generation tax free.

> 2) **Qualified Plans.** These techniques use pension funds and the like to create assets that will not be taxed, either during the life of the farm owner or on his death.

> 3) **Family "Banks."** These are various approaches to loaning cash to non-farm heirs and letting them make their money in other ventures.

These sophisticated techniques, like brain surgery, are best not practiced on yourself. They require experienced, competent advice.

Still, even in tough situations, a buy/sell can do a lot. It could, in the above example, define under what terms and conditions a buy out would be accomplished. Possibly, life insurance could fund part of the buy out, with the balance being paid in installments to the sisters over a defined period. Money could be set aside in pension plans to go to the non-farm heirs. Gifts of non-voting interest could be given to the non-farm heirs. There are many options.

The important point is that, even in tough situations, a buy/sell, properly written, can prevent forced sales and family squabbles.

The main ideas to take away from all this are three:

> 1) *Estate planning needn't be complex.*

> 2) *It must be started early, maybe even as early as today.*

3) *Trained professional advisors are essential parts of the process.*

Why should we put all those years of sweat, blood, effort, and courage into building the family farm, only to leave its disposition to strangers? It doesn't have to happen that way.

Chapter 15
GETTING HELP — AND WHY

There once was a broadcasting company that owned some television stations. Those TV stations had a net worth of about $20 million, and that year generated $200 million in income.

That's a "return on assets" ratio of 10 to 1.

It might be on the high end, but ratios in this range are relatively common in the successful in-town business.

For the family farm, on the other hand, the ratio usually goes very far the other way. A cartoon that appeared in *Ohio Farmer* recently showed a farmer talking to a lottery official. The official asked the farmer what he would do if he won a million dollars in the state lottery.

> *"I'd use the money to farm with,"* the farmer answered, *"and I'd keep farming until the money was gone."*

Most successful farmers have tremendous asset values, with an income that's relatively small compared to those assets.

So, why do so many keep farming? Well, as many farm

owners have said to us, "Sure, I know I could retire tomorrow, sell the farm, and move to town. I'd have lots more income than I have right now. But that's okay. I'm farming because farming's what I want to do."

This is the crux of the problem in farming. Lots of people have *proved* that they would spend their whole year farming and not make any money, just for the opportunity to do it again the following year. It's a plain fact. Many family farmers are in agriculture for reasons that go far beyond the desire to make money.

FARMING'S BECOME BIG BUSINESS

Not too long ago, this wasn't the case. When land values were skyrocketing, farmers were at least making money on paper, even if they didn't take out a lot of cash at the end of the year. They were able to borrow money to buy more land because they couldn't lose. Borrowing the money at 6% and 8%, and investing it in an asset that was growing by 10% to 15%, was just too good a deal to pass up.

Today, that's all changed. Far fewer banks are loaning money based on the assets of the operation. Few, if any, are loaning based on the potential rise in the value of the farm.

More and more, banks are loaning money based on income and a supportable projection of how the loan can be repaid. This is a key change in perspective.

As financing decisions depend more and more on how well the operation does in income, more and more farmers are going to (and will have to) turn their eyes to the business and financial management side of their farm operations. As they do this, an increasing number of them will find themselves making decisions on the basis of things like cash flow or profitability, rather than on "that's what we've always grown" or "that's the way Dad did it."

The "entrepreneurial" side of the farmer may be very strong and have a lot of potential, but it is largely undeveloped. He's always been able to base his success on his "productive" side, leaving entrepreneurship to its own devices.

Take the Christmas tree business as an example. There's going to be a tremendous shake out in that business over the next few years. Millions and millions of trees have been planted that will not have a home when they're full-grown, and this glut is going to drive the price of trees down. That means that some Christmas tree growers are not going to survive.

According to reports we've seen, the key to success in the Christmas tree business has only 25% to do with how good the tree is and how well it's grown. The other three-quarters has to do with the ability to market the tree and develop distribution channels.

In July, while one grower is spending his time driving around on vacation in another part of the country, his competitor may be out calling on service clubs, lining up next season's customers. It is easy to imagine which of the two of those businesses will be around in the long run.

PROFITABILITY VS. PRODUCTIVITY

The term "entrepreneurial farming" is arising with increasing frequency in the farm journals and magazines. What does this refer to? It refers to people who happen to be so geographically positioned that they can raise specialty crops, start roadside markets, and sell produce directly to supermarkets instead of the usual method of selling through wholesalers.

Many factors enhance the profitability of this kind of operation, but they are good examples of an unusual state of affairs — *profitable* productivity. There's a crying need for outside help and analysis to enhance profitability. There is a need for people to come in and work with farmers to help them determine which enterprises to invest in, and in what way.

Not many of these experts exist. The people from the extension service, and the like, have performed miracles getting production up. Now, there's a crying need for more interaction between colleges of agriculture and business schools, to help the successful farmer be more *profitable* on his own scale.

Many today are already taking that perspective. We have a number of clients growing Christmas trees or fruits and vegetables, who know they may have three to eight years after purchase of land and the planting of crops before they see the required $.10 coming back from the $1 investment.

Clearly, these people wouldn't take this risk, wouldn't invest money in largely non-deductible expansion, if they weren't interested in the long-term growth of the business and future income. They would simply take that same money and put it in the bank and have income from it immediately.

No, they think much of the time in the long term. They are, in fact, better than anyone else at being willing to do things for the long-term good, of themselves as well as of the nation. They just haven't built *profit* into that long-term picture.

This must change — and it *can* change. But only with more interaction between the business college and the agricultural college, indeed, between the whole business sector and the farm sector. With this kind of help, farmers can become as well educated about the techniques of making a profit as they are about the techniques of feeding the world.

Maybe, if farmers become better business managers, the rest of us will have to get used to paying higher prices for the food we eat.

We have no reason to complain. Maybe we can survive losing our steel industry to poor management. Maybe. But if we lose agriculture, or it becomes controlled by only a few because the family farm disappears, we are in real trouble.

MANAGING A BIG BUSINESS

Most farmers don't see themselves as business people. They're *farmers*. The more successful among them don't even see themselves as "big" farmers, because most of them know other people who are even bigger than they are.

A year or so ago, the wife of one of our clients said over the phone:

> "Boy, it hasn't been a great year. As a matter of fact, we lost $50,000." She was quiet for a minute and then she said, "But you know, I was

*talking to one of our friends out in California, and
they told me they'd lost $390,000. So I guess
things aren't that bad for us."*

The same thing works when it comes to profits. We make
some money, but others seem to make more. Most family farmers know someone bigger than they are, so even if their operation is worth several million dollars and grossing tremendous
amounts of money, the amount of their *net* is generally small,
small enough, at least, to keep them from feeling they're significant *business* people.

The result of this is yet another contradiction. Successful
farmers don't always act like the business people they are. They
don't seek help. They don't think that they need any "fancy"
accountants or any "big time" lawyers to do anything for them
because, after all, they're just small farmers.

We were talking with a client the other day, a fellow who
had several hundred acres of vegetables, from pickles to cabbage to potatoes. He was looking over his operation and said:

*"You know, I'm always surprised when
people come by here and ask how I manage this
big business. We just started here and took the
various vegetables on one at a time. It's no big
thing. After 30-plus years of doing this, the farming aspect has become automatic. There are simply certain times when you harvest different crops
and certain ways of marketing and doing the
farming. There's nothing 'big' about this operation."*

In a sense, he was right. Whether you are farming 150
acres or 15,000 acres, the farming "technology" is essentially
the same. But where he was wrong was in his failure to recognize
that his is a big business and needs to be treated like the capital-
intensive operation it is, one that may have millions of dollars
worth of assets and just as much liability.

Farm owners are becoming aware that "gross" is not "net,"

particularly in agriculture. In farming, there's very little slippage, very little spread between the cost of doing business and the value of the product sold. Any little glitch in the program can turn a good year into a disaster.

Yet most successful farmers we've come across are farming largely by the seat of their pants, and they've been doing it that way for the past 30 years or so.

Don't get us wrong — that's a considerable "seat." Each year they go to the various schools provided by the extension services, and a little bit of knowledge is added incrementally to their total storehouse of farming wisdom. During the winter, they may take courses at the local ag college. But generally speaking, those courses are not finance, marketing, accounting, or business courses. They are yet more production-related courses.

Farm owners are very conscientious about keeping abreast of what's going on agriculturally. The problem is that since they've never been taught to be managers, they don't act like managers. Each year they get a little further behind, almost unnoticeably, like creeping blindness.

A client once said to us:

> *"Look, we've done the planning. We've protected the family. We've set things up so that one of our farms is in the hands of the boys and secured. Now leave me alone because I'm going to run this other farm the way I want to whether anybody likes it or not!"*

Another client worked with us for a number of years putting together a sound estate plan. It provided benefits to the widow should he die. It secured the farm heirs, who'd have the security of knowing that the farm would continue and that they'd end up with it. There'd be security for the non-farm heirs in knowing that they'd ultimately get their inheritance in a form they could use.

All of these things were great — and fine with him. However, what really motivated him to put it all together was something else entirely. He knew if he agreed to do the planning, we'd all leave him alone to do what he wanted to do — run his farm and his canning company. And he was 75 years old at the time!

To a great extent, modernizing the business operations of the farm is the job of the younger generation, sometimes in spite of Dad, sometimes with his tacit agreement, and sometimes, of course, with his enthusiastic approval.

But rarely is he the one who pushes to get it done. Important as business planning is for succession, he has too much farm work to do (which, coincidentally, is also what he *likes* to do).

This is why he so desperately needs help.

WHY DAD NEEDS HELP

The fact is, no farmer, no matter how successful, no matter how brilliant, no matter how hard working, can do his planning by himself. He needs someone with the interest to encourage him, the sensitivity not to add to his problems, and the training to show him practical answers.

Long-range planning is a crucial factor in being an effective, successful farmer, but it's probably a very strange concept to Dad. He usually only believes in work, hard work, and more of it. It's what he demands of himself. It's what he demands out of his successors. Help, to him, is working hard alongside of him, yet that's not the kind of help he needs. There's nothing in hard work to guarantee effectiveness, and even if there were a guarantee, there's usually no real way to measure it.

What's the standard of doing a good job, after all? There's Dad's measure, of course, but his standard is sweat, which is input rather than outcome: "We just aren't working hard enough." As far as he's concerned, there's no *time* for "looking ahead." There's too much to do right now.

His successors aren't in much better shape. By the time the flood of work overflows the dikes, some of the fun goes out of the family farm as a career. They can't seem to get Dad's respect, his direct commitment to succession, or any information on his plans for them (if, indeed, he has any).

The farm seems buried, disorganized. It's run according to crisis management. In all the dust and noise, their ideas are ignored — and when those ideas are ignored long enough, you can be sure their spouses are losing faith in the possibility of it all working out.

The mighty family farm's engine is racing. The tach is almost redlined. The hatches are screwed down. The windows are rolled up. Everybody's frustrated, waiting to go somewhere, *wanting* to go somewhere, but nobody knows quite how to get the family farm's succession planning in gear.

If only we could just *ask* somebody . . .

WHY DAD WON'T ASK FOR HELP

Remember that one of the great advantages of owning one's own farm is privacy. By staying our own boss, we can make sure nobody knows "nuttin," and keep it that way.

This is a Good Thing, right?

In some ways, yes. It depends on one's point of view. If privacy in and of itself is the major objective, then the absence of "nosy," "pushy" questioners *would* be a Good Thing. On the other hand, if continuity, succession, growth, and profitability are the major goals — as we've assumed all along they are — lack of outside help and review is everything *but* a Good Thing. It's an open invitation to agricultural suicide.

For today's family farm to succeed, generation to generation, someone must teach the managers to stay afloat, then to swim — and maybe help a little with fighting off all the sharks and barracudas.

Trouble is, too many family farms are "closed" companies — in fact as much as in legal terminology. Truth is, they're "hermetically sealed" companies.

Few have any outside review of management judgments, decisions, or policies. And far too few have available to them any expertise, knowledge, or advice other than what they get from insiders — the *same* insiders who've been drawing on the *same* experiences over and over again for a generation.

This doesn't happen because farm owners can't afford outside help. It happens because the insiders like things that way. The very thought of having some outsider poking around in the business books tends to make the family farmer's every bodily aperture pucker up with indignation.

When we asked one crusty farmer, 74, about his assets, he told us he had $300,000 in high-interest certificates of deposit. Then we asked what he planned for that money after his death.

> *"Son, I didn't have anybody help me make this money,"* he answered, *"and I sure don't need someone to help me decide what to do with it."*

This strong sense of independence doesn't mean successful farmers don't ask for input to their decisions. They do — but only from very carefully selected, fundamentally "safe" sources, like his friends down at the coffee shop who share his problems and his prejudices. (But not his information. They only get to know what he decides to tell them, which is usually very little.)

Who are these "sources"? Well, Dad, himself, of course. He runs the show very well, thank you, and makes sure everybody knows it. But who else? A few key inside managers, maybe, as well as the oldest son — within some severe limits.

At least Dad has his professional advisors, you're probably thinking — his attorney, accountant, banker, insurance underwriter, and so forth. At least they're around to keep him out of trouble.

But are they? Really?

Actually, his asking for help from his advisors isn't any more likely than his showing the balance sheet to his successors. In the first place, Dad doesn't have a lot of respect for professional advisors. In the second place, their fee meters are always running, and much too fast. Because of the fees they charge, Dad isn't about to use them for casual advice or informal brainstorming.

Unfortunately, the advisors don't often help matters much, either. They go along with Old Dad, passively accepting the fact that he doesn't use them as he should.

"He's just that way. He's stubborn. He's tough. He's not about to listen to anybody."

"We can recommend," they tend to say in understandable rationalization, *"but it's up to him to accept our advice. We can't force him."*

Many farm owners, just like their in-town counterparts, use a special technique with their advisors. We call it "divide and conquer." Although it isn't done consciously, Dad plays his advisors off against each other, meets with them individually, tells them only what they "need to know," then accepts only the advice his gut tells him is right. Essentially, he goes through the motions of seeking advice, but only accepts his own.

The result of all this play-acting and rationalization can be seen in the dusty, unsigned estate plan, the inadequate accounting system, the poorly administered pension fund, the confused insurance setup, and the lack of sophisticated cash management and financing.

Dad, you see, does all these things himself. His business is "different." He's going to get around to his estate plan, even has some thoughts on it, but economic conditions are forcing him to spend all of his waking hours keeping afloat.

His accounting system was "carefully evolved" to fit his unique situation ("My business is different"). He's not about to let some *banker* manage his money ("He never took a risk in his life"), and insurance is a game that agents play with him to raise their commissions ("I always buy term").

Dad is used to being good at what he does. He quite easily confuses talent with success and success with infallibility. If he did it so well in vegetables, wheat, dairy herds, or turkeys, then who better to do just as well in estate planning, accounting, finance, and management in general?

All he really needs is a little more time — maybe when his heirs have more of a handle on things, and Dad can spend more time on policy decisions. Know any good books?

Of course, the kids never really get a handle on things, and Old Dad never really finds the time to handle all of these planning matters.

But don't worry. He will. He will. When things settle down.

At least Dad has his "board of directors" to go to. Right?

What board? This is a partnership, or a proprietorship. There's no board. True — but even if Dad were incorporated, as most in-town family businesses are, he still wouldn't have a board. Not a real one.

Oh, Dad's got a group of old friends and cronies who meet sort of like a board. This is his "Coffee Shop Board," those friends who've heard about his problems over the years, as he's heard about theirs. He's also got his partners. They talk about a lot of things. They complain. They tell a few old stories.

And that's usually about all they do.

These people don't help. They commiserate.

OPENING THE DOORS TO "THE BEST"

So where does the successful farmer go for help? He walks out into the pasture and looks up into the clouds. *Please, Lord, what can I do?* And The Lord looks down on him with pity and sorrow, and replies: *"Gosh, it beats me!"*

If Dad and the successors wanted just one technique, one sure-cure miracle "drug" that could solve their problems, the closest they could come is the elimination of their isolation.

Far too many family farms are fortresses with rusted chains and jammed drawbridges. Sure, farming is a solitary occupation — but it doesn't have to be lonely. Solitude means freedom and creativity. Loneliness is just plain bad business.

But who could make it "unlonely"?

People who could help. People who make it their business — as the farmer makes farming his — to solve problems like those the farmer faces.

In spite of the successful farmer's cynicism:

- There ARE **bankers** who understand farming and actually want the farmer to succeed.

- There ARE **accountants** who've seen the insides of hundreds of agricultural and farming businesses, who know which management systems work and which don't.

- There ARE **attorneys** who have a broad range of techniques at their fingertips for solving management and ownership transition problems.

- There ARE **insurance agents** who know that the products they sell do, in fact, solve a lot of the farmer's estate problems, and will sell only what will do the job.

- There ARE **planners** who can help bring all these people together to help design an integrated plan.

We know these people exist because we work with them every day. They are just as good at what they do as the farmer is at what he does. Yet, he doesn't use them.

Why? Well, he's cheap, of course — but then most of us are. And maybe he's been burned by bad advice and service, but one bad animal shouldn't condemn the whole herd. He's uncomfortable with these in-town types, but then he was probably uncomfortable with Mom when he first met her. That didn't keep them from getting together.

He's shy, too. *Why,* he asks himself, *would the really top-notch people want to mess with a little operation like mine?* Because that's precisely the reason they're in business, to work with people like him and operations like his.

Finally, he feels he's unqualified to recognize the best advisors. *Heck,* he thinks, *the only way I can be sure what they're telling me is right is to know as much as they do.*

HOW TO FIND THEM

There's no reason why a successful farmer has to know as much as the advisor in order to judge his advice. All he needs is a way to find the best. It sounds tough, but it needn't be. The key, simply, is to go out looking for the best.

Really, he's done it many times before. How does a farmer find the best extension agent? How does he find the best veterinarian, or dairy consultant, or feed and fertilizer supplier? He looks around. He asks other farmers whose opinions he respects. Who do you use? Is he or she any good? Would you recommend them?

Pretty soon, certain names start coming up again and again. And those who are recommended by the most people, who have the best reputations, are the people selected by the successful farmer. If they do well for him, he recommends them to others.

The same exact procedure applies to professional advice.

Yet few farmers go out and actively seek good advisors. Instead, they wait until strangers knock on their doors. No wonder they're suspicious. If not this, they just stick with the people they've used for years. That's okay if they're doing the job, but for so many successful farmers, they're not doing the job. Trouble is, it's easier for busy Old Dad to stick with the old cronies than to go out and change.

It may seem we're oversimplifying when we say that to find good advisors, go out and look for them. But we're not. It is, in fact, the answer.

Try it. You'll be surprised. Your future will have a better chance of being successful, and your family will be grateful.

And maybe farming can get back to the fun it used to be.

Postscript
WORKING IT OUT

THE MACKEY FAMILY

The Problems:

- How to survive very high estate taxes
- How to bring children in fairly
- How to fund Dad's retirement
- How to recognize oldest son's contribution
- How to be fair to off-farm daughter

The Solutions:

- New wills and marital deduction trusts
- Incorporation of operating and land holding assets
- Recapitalization with non-voting preferred stock
- Moving growth to common stock
- A gifting program for the preferred stock
- Buy/sell agreements among on-farm heirs
- A salary continuation plan for Dad

. . . *(CONTINUED FROM THE PREFACE)* The analysis of the Mackey's problem was based on the present worth of their business, as well as its projected worth, computed using different assumptions for inflation, growth and so forth. Based on the tax situation at the time, their advisors determined that there would be a large tax bill at the death of either Harold or Helen and recommended that *new wills and marital deduction trusts* be put in place.

Under the laws then in existence, had death occurred, there would have been a substantial savings with this approach — a savings which would've grown larger and larger during the passing years.

Further, because of the rapidly appreciating farmland and the various goals and objectives, it was recommended by their lawyer that the farm be *incorporated*. This corporation would be more than just an operating corporation, it would also be a land holding company, since the land represented the greatest and most volatile value of the operation.

All of the land, machinery and equipment was placed into the corporation, and stock was issued. Two kinds of stock were issued. The first type, stock which represented about 90% of the value of the business, was *non-voting preferred stock*. This stock would not go up in value and it would receive preferential treatment in case of liquidation. This meant that the owners would receive their money first, and it would pay a fixed dividend each year.

This non-voting preferred stock was issued to Harold and Helen because they owned the vast majority of the assets being placed in this new business. The boys received some preferred stock to cover the growth they had produced, and an amount of preferred stock that recognized their accrued past years' earnings.

In this way, recognition was given to Greg's $90,000 of onion money so that in the future he could redeem that stock, if so desired, by selling it back to the corporation to get his cash.

Common stock was also issued. This is where all of the future appreciation of the business would take place. We could compare this stock combination to a pressure cooker with the lid representing the preferred stock and the escape valve representing the common. When inflationary or growth pressure is put on the farm business, the escape valve opens, and that increase in value accrues to the owners of the common stock.

The common stock was gifted to all three boys because, by then, two of them were out of college and the third would be soon.

The preferred stock was also used, and can continue to be used, as a vehicle for gifting. Under current tax law, outright gifts of $10,000 each year from Harold and $10,000 from Helen can be given to as many people as they want. These gifts, when given in preferred stock, reduce their estate by the amount of the gift, but do so without any cash changing hands.

In this manner, a large amount of money can be given over to the next generation over a period of years without any tax cost being incurred, and without the loss of use of any capital.

As it's turned out, gifts were only made one year, because after that the land values started to level off and have since declined somewhat. For this reason, the need to make gifts has diminished. All this may change in the future, and if so they'll be ready.

In the Mackey's case, the same thing could have been accomplished with a limited partnership and a few other structures, but the corporate route was chosen by their attorney, their accountant, and other advisors because of the need to do some major income tax planning, and to make use of some of the other benefits that a corporation offers.

Five years have gone by since the completion of this plan. Three tax law changes have occurred, which have, to a large extent lessened the estate tax burden and in every single case have made those original plans more sensible.

Dave and Tim have now married, and all three boys have children. All three Mackey sons are in the farm business and share equally in the growth of the operation. While land values have remained constant for the most part, the value of the common stock has gone up considerably because debt has been retired.

Amy has decided not to pursue a retailing career. She is married to a boy who was one of her boyfriends in high school. Interestingly enough, he has a farm background and even though she swore it wouldn't happen, he is involved in their farm business. As a matter of fact, she works there part time herself. They have no children, yet.

Just recently, the three boys agreed to a simple stock transfer plan to include their brother-in-law, Joe. They've each agreed to give outright a small amount of their stock to Joe each year over the next several years, so that he will ultimately own a significant part of the operation — and therefore take part in the growth.

They told us they agreed to this because they know Joe is going to be a substantial contributor to the profits, and will, therefore, be a key manager like them. They believe they can continue to grow the business so that it can sustain all four of their families the way it supported all of them as they were growing up.

A salary continuation plan was designed by their lawyer to provide an income for Harold after retirement. While this is an expense to the operation, they all reasoned that much of the money Harold made over the years was plowed back into the business. As a result of this reinvestment, Dad didn't have much in savings toward retirement.

(A telling incident about these young men was a conversation we had about the 20-year salary continuation plan first presented to them. They'd thought about it awhile, and when we visited a few weeks later with their lawyer, the only provision they didn't like was the "20 years." What happens, they asked, if Dad lives more than 20 years? Will he be out of money? We drew up a new plan which will provide income for Harold for as long as he lives, and then for Mom as long as she lives.)

A *buy/sell agreement* was established originally that is being revised as the situation changes. This buy/sell agreement provides for the orderly purchase of the business interest owned by one brother by either the remaining brothers or by the farm itself. Funds for this were provided by life insurance policies on their lives. Because the boys are relatively young, insurance was a relatively inexpensive option.

Now, should something happen to one of the brothers, the widow of that deceased brother would receive full value for her husband's interest in the business and, yet, the remaining brothers would not have to be in business with her in the future. Similarly, if one brother wants out, there is provision for that, too.

THE PAUL FAMILY

The Problems:

- How to handle too many interested heirs
- How to recognize oldest son's contribution
- How to handle explosive growth in business value

The Solutions:

- Definition of partnership between father and son to shift deductions and income
- Limited partnership to recognize difference in contribution
- Place surplus heirs in other operations
- A buy/sell agreement between father and sons

. . . After much discussion, it became clear that it really wasn't Garth's idea to give up the business and turn it over to the boys, not immediately, anyway. That wasn't his real problem. The problem was he just didn't know how he could eventually make the transition happen with all the growth they were experiencing.

Also, during this time, he was faced with some difficult estate taxation laws, and the value of the farmland in his particular locale was rising rapidly.

The advisors met with the various family members and began to systematically determine each of their objectives. They learned that Ruth really wanted the boys to work together on the farm. Garth wanted to make sure that he and Ruth had an income and had some opportunity for growth, but, fortunately, they were financially comfortable. So if he started to divest himself of some of it, it wouldn't be a problem for him — as long as he could have some *say* in the matter.

One problem, because of the tremendous amounts of investment tax credit and depreciation that were being thrown off by the farm, was that Garth was not paying any appreciable amount of income tax. On the other hand, since Tom didn't have any real deductions, and was getting all of his income in the form of wages, he was paying a very high percentage of his income in taxes.

The first step was to define a *partnership arrangement* between Tom and Garth which would allow for a shifting of deductions and income between the two of them. That, for all practical purposes, eliminated income taxes for them both. Looking at the family enterprise as a whole, the dollars saved in income taxes were seen as a substantial portion of the income needed to bring Kevin into the operation.

Kevin has now been in the partnership for three years, and the total tax liability has not been increased over what it had been originally when it was all borne by Tom as an employee.

The third son, Ron, delayed his entrance into the farm for two years by going to a technical college to learn mechanics. He had always been very good at mechanics, and it was generally felt that this would be an area where he could make a significant contribution to the farm operation.

To the extent that different family members have expertise, training, desire, and knowledge in different aspects of the business operation, everyone can benefit without stepping on one another's toes.

In any event, during the two years that he was at the technical school, the farm business grew so that when he did come back, it was able to absorb him without any strain. Additional fruit trees had been planted and were now coming into production. The tax planning that was being done by their CPA, and this additional production, as well as the savings realized by doing their own maintenance made his entrance into the business easy.

But it was the opinion of their advisors that to add any more people to the business would be more than the farm could bear at that time. It was now time to test that, however, because the fourth son had graduated from high school. He had no interest in continuing his education, and was ready for the work force.

Fortunately, another client, the Leberts (discussed below), had a situation where they needed someone just like Jeff because their own son was not going to be involved in the farm business. Now Jeff works for the Leberts, and has done so for the past two years. Assuming things continue to go as they are, it looks as though a buy/sell agreement will be entered into whereby Jeff will eventually own a substantial portion or all of that farm's business. But that's the Lebert's story.

To continue with the Pauls, one of the overriding concerns was recognizing Tom's 10-year contribution to the business, particularly since his brother was just then coming in.

A *limited partnership* was used to recognize his contribution through the partnership share distribution. Similar to the Mackey's preferred stock technique, the entire partnership was frozen in value at its organization with future growth to be divided among Garth, Tom, Kevin, and Ron, the newly arrived son.

In this way, Garth and Tom had an asset base based on their previous contributions, but future growth was divided into thirds to include Kevin, and, later, fourths with the entrance of Ron.

This created a situation where Garth has 25% of the voice in the business, so he still has some say. Actually, of course, he still has 100% control since the boys typically do what their father suggests.

Most important, Garth now receives only 25% of the growth, which now is almost equivalent to 100% of the growth that was taking place before the business expansion. Because of the new estate tax laws, and with some new estate planning techniques, taxes at his or Ruth's death will not present an insurmountable problem.

Also, because these limited partnership shares are fixed, they throw off income so he has an income base which will accrue to him and Ruth and be paid to them in retirement. Therefore, their retirement needs are being handled.

Planning, under the watchful eyes of competent advisors, has made possible the succession of this business from one generation to the next, one family to three families. The fourth son is moving onto another farm operation and the remaining son, who is still in school, is not decided yet.

The business will probably be big enough to absorb him, too, but it's unlikely he'll want to come in. More likely, he'll end up working with his brother in the Lebert orchard operation. It is possible, in short, for the Paul family to end up with two major farm businesses without asking all five brothers to work together for the rest of their lives.

All of this planning has been done without any unnecessary income taxes and without the payment of any unnecessary estate taxes. To the extent that the boys and their dad are involved in the business together, a *buy/sell agreement*, appropriately funded with life insurance, has been drafted to provide for the buy out of one another's interest in the event of death.

It seems that all the bases have been covered, as long as these people can continue to work together as friends as well as family. Something they've managed very well up to now.

THE LEBERT FAMILY

The Problem:

- How to handle the lack of interested heirs

The Solutions:

- Bring in non-family successor
- Draft a mutually beneficial employment contract
- Carefully defined stock options for non-family suc-

cessor, with restrictions, to liquidate present
owners and their heirs

- Profit sharing plan to fund tax on options

. . . Part of the solution for the Leberts, as indicated just
above, was the Paul family. One of the older Paul boys was doing
some field work on a custom basis for Russell Lebert, so Mr.
Lebert knew of the family.

As a result of the work we were doing for the Paul family,
it became apparent that Jeff, the fourth son, would not have a
place in the family business because of size and opportunity
constraints. We then introduced Jeff to the Leberts, suggesting
that a relationship be established whereby the Leberts con-
tracted with Jeff to work for them for two years before any type
of permanent business relationship was established.

That two years has come and gone and now an *employment contract* exists between the Lebert orchards and Jeff. The
gist of this agreement is that each year that Jeff stays there and
works he will be given *stock options* in the farm corporation.

These options are subject to restrictions. The restrictions
provide that, should he leave for any reason other than death
or disability, he will forfeit these options and in that way the
options are not taxable to him until the restrictions are removed.

A schedule has been set up for the removal of these restrictions. In this way, Ron will have the income from the farm
operation through the *profit sharing plan* to pay the tax on the
stock options as the restrictions are removed, and he will ultimately receive one third of the stock in the farm corporation in
this manner.

The other two thirds of the stock will be bought by him
from Russell and Alice Lebert, or from their heirs at their death
or before.

This is to ensure that the Lebert children will receive
their proportion of the inheritance based on the value of the
Lebert orchards when this program was established, and it assures that Jeff will have ⅓ of the interest based on his time and
service. It also makes sure that part of the appreciation in the
value of the business will accrue to Jeff, should he decide to stay

on and run the farm in the next generation.

The Leberts today are going through a plan revision, because the size of the business has grown substantially under Russell and Jeff's direction. It now appears that Jeff's younger brother may be coming into the business after high school and will work there during the time that he is in the agricultural technical college. If this youngest Paul decides to become involved in the Lebert operation long-term, a mechanism will be needed to ensure that he can share in the business appreciation, also.

The purpose of all this planning is the transfer of the business through one generation to the next with the least amount of tax cost. The objective was to avoid unnecessary payments, while balancing the senior Leberts' need for a return on their investment, and the younger Leberts' right to a fair inheritance.

Naturally, the Paul boys are interested in having a business opportunity that provides them both present and future benefits. The plan that was developed took all these various needs into account.

THE GRANGERS

The Problems:

- How to handle ownership transfer to cousins
- How to handle different numbers of heirs between owning families

The Solutions:

- Formation of a holding corporation and an operating partnership
- Severing the joint ownership of the brothers
- Freezing holdings of each brother
- Moving appreciation to trusts for heirs
- Drafting a buy/sell between two brothers
- Employment contract with son-in-law

. . . The Granger situation was somewhat unique. Because of some estate planning considerations a *family farm cor-*

poration was formed to freeze the value of the Grangers' underlying assets for tax purposes, and these securities could be used as gifts to the farm and non-farm heirs in order to reduce the estate and pass on assets to the next generation. However, for purposes of operating the business, a *partnership* made the most sense for the Granger brothers from an income tax point of view.

To attack the Grangers' first worry, that they'd be forcing their heirs to work together, all of *the joint ownership of the two brothers was severed* so that each brother owned his particular portion of the real estate outright in his own name.

Because of the geographical nature of the various parcels, the types of perennial and annual crops that were grown on those parcels, and how they were related to the rest of the operation, the land was divided in such a way that two businesses could exist separately from one another, with the possible exception of some of the barns and storage facilities.

In this way, during Jack and Dale's life, or during the next generation, the business could be easily (relatively) separated, and this would provide an escape valve for the next or the present generation.

The holdings of each brother were placed in their individual family corporations, which were structured in such a way that some values were frozen and others were left to appreciate. The values that were frozen were given to Jack and his wife, Bev, and Dale and his wife, Nancy, respectively. The appreciating values were placed either outright or in *trust* in the hands of the next generation.

In this way, appreciation in the business was placed in the next generation without loss of control on the part of Jack and Dale — and without any cash changing hands. NO taxes were payable as a result of this technique, either.

A *buy/sell agreement* was drafted, which would, at the death of the senior generation, provide a means for the farm heirs to ultimately end up with all of the farm assets, and the non-farm heirs would receive their inheritance in cash. In this way, because there is only one boy in each of the two families, the balance of power would remain the same into the next generation.

A partnership was established to operate the business, and the two partners would be the respective family farm corporations. The partnership would own certain assets relative to the ongoing operation of the business and would maintain a tax position that, should a dissolution become the goal, the assets could be distributed without any particular tax problem, and the partnership could be dissolved leaving two separate businesses.

Even though there has been a general downturn in agriculture from the standpoint of land values, this has not occurred in this particular farm operation because of its location close to market, the crops raised, the type of soil, the general location and so forth. Still, it hasn't appreciated like before, either. Because debt has been paid down and because values have appreciated somewhat, we have experienced a substantial shift of value to the next generation that is presently on the farm without a penny's worth of gift or other taxes being paid.

The organization is now flexible enough to absorb a son-in-law peacefully. Through an *employment contract*, non-qualified stock options, etc., means have been established to give him ownership, while protecting the family farm.

With these options, if he wants to be a part of the business long-term, he can buy stock in the operation or he can be given stock in the business or a combination of both can be implemented. This way, he and his wife will be able to participate in the future of the operation.

Should something happen to their relationship or should he leave for any reason, there will be a mandatory buy-back on the part of the corporation. While this would allow the corporation to be made whole again, it also provides compensation to this son-in-law for his efforts on behalf of the business.

INDEX